Love Nots

Searching for the Love Only
God Could Give

Ramona Lyons

i

Love Nots

Love Nots

Love Nots

Searching for the Love Only God Could Give

Ramona Lyons

Kingdom Scribes Publishing, LLC.

Love Nots

Love NOTS

ISBN 978-0-692-94562-9

Kingdom Scribes Publishing, LLC.
Kingdomscribespublishing@yahoo.com
www.kingdom-scribes.com

iv

Love Nots

Table of Contents

Love Nots

Words from the Author

The purpose of this book is to encourage a relationship with Christ, and bring empowerment and encouragement to women. I want to use my testimony as a catalyst, to help and give hope, to those who are in despair. I want my story to help single women, and single mothers. I also want to share my experiences, to display the love and glory of God in my life. In order for this to occur, I know that I will have to uncover some of the most painful events of my life. The events and occurrences in my life that has affected me the most.

In this process, and in the unveiling of these events, I would like to convey, how God and his love, brought me out of a dark and horrible pit and delivered me from my circumstances. How I could rise above the turmoil and the ashes and become the woman that God has called me to be. I understand the pain of being rejected all too well, for I have been rejected my entire life. By first and foremost my father. Through the process of writing this book, I was forced to rehash, and remember painful experiences that I had suppressed that resurfaced painful and bitter emotions. This was very therapeutic for me because I was able to really deal with it and allow God to heal me.

As a result of that initial rejection, a seed was planted at a very young age, which in turn made me attracted to men who also rejected me. This cycle went on and on for years. The generational curse of bad and truly awful relationships, did its best to diminish the love that I had for myself. I didn't know who I truly was. I didn't know that God loved me or just how much.

I continually found myself in relationships where men demeaned me and used me. I allowed these men to attack my self-esteem. This left me feeling inadequate and unworthy. I believed in my mind, that I was not worthy of anyone's love. I would give more and more of myself trying so desperately to receive the love I was in search of, to fill a void that only Jesus Christ could fill. However, once I began to come into the revelation of God's love, my life tremendously changed. This revelation of unconditional love was the beginning of my foundation.

Prelude

Daddy's Love

The earliest memory I have, is when I was 4 years old. My mother had recently moved into her first flat and was having a house party. I remember hearing laughing and talking in the other room. My brother and I were in our room. The room was only big enough to fit one bed. Though we were supposed to be asleep, we were listening in on the adults, as you know children do. All of a sudden, I hear my Grandmother's voice. I could hear her cussing up a storm. She and my mother were arguing.

I just remember her saying, "Where is Miki?" The curtain was drawn back, because we didn't have a door. Grandma pulled back the curtain, swooped me up and we left. She didn't take my brother Mari, he was just a little baby. He may have just turned a year old. She took me to live with her that night. My Grandmother has always been present in my life. She was there from the very beginning. I recall that particular moment, as her initial presence and influence in my life.

Alice Carol Calhoun was and is "The Matriarch" of our family. She helped raise me from an infant. I was the first grandchild, the baby, and I was spoiled—rotten. It wasn't too long before my mom was living with *us*, and eventually the entire family. Our address was 8900 Dexter Avenue. There was a lot of history in that house. I lived there with my Grandmother, my mom Laura, my Aunts Loretta (Bunnie), Allene and my Uncle John Jr.

My parents were not married and my father was always in and out of my life. Sometimes months and even years would pass, before I would see or even hear from him. He was constantly in and out of jail during my childhood. But that didn't matter to me. When he would show up, I would be so happy to see him. Because even if it was for a short time, I was still daddy's little girl. I yearned for love and acceptance from my father. He always made me feel loved and special when he came around. He would pick me up and tell me how pretty I was and kiss me on my cheeks. It was just so sporadic when I saw him. The lapse in times started to get longer and longer.

Many times, he would visit, it was unexpected, never scheduled. Sometimes I could hear my mom arguing with him on the phone. Saying, "It's too dog on late, why are you calling at 10:00 at night to see Miki?" Yes, I know what that was about now. My mother believed I was an afterthought to him. Maybe he was in the neighborhood at the time and just happened to remember he had a daughter. Who really knows? After several minutes of rehashed history and arguing, she would give in and let him see me.

It was obvious my mother and father didn't get along. The first half of our visits, she would watch intensely from the dining room, monitoring his every move, his every gesture. As if he was going to bolt for the door with me or something. She watched, waiting to object to anything that he would say that she felt was a lie. He could tell some stories though, he was a good liar. All the promises that was made to me as a child, promises of taking me on trips and shopping, I knew they were lies. What he failed to realize was that I didn't care about material things. All I cared about was him. So, I would listen and pretend to believe him.

My mother didn't want him feeding my head with a bunch of lies and false promises. So, by the time the visits were over, they would be in a full-blown argument. I did not understand growing up, why she hated him so much. She always had this intense gaze of resentment in her eyes. Words unspoken, yet spoke so profoundly. Perhaps he'd broken her heart one too many times. My father would always make light of the situation and her attitude toward him, as if it was nothing or suggesting that she still had feelings for him. I remember hearing, "Girl your mama still loves me."

He always made extremely cocky statements, which only made it worse. Remember that song by The Pretenders, "It's a thin line between love and hate?" That song described them perfectly! Maybe she did love and hate him at the same time. Or maybe she just hated the fact that she loved him. I was informed that he did break her heart. When they met they were both teenagers attending Northwestern high school in Detroit. My mom was beautiful, smart, and could dance, but was a no nonsense young lady.

I was informed that she played hard to get for a long time, but he liked her and loved the chase. Perhaps she knew he was no good for her and desperately tried to fight her feelings for him. However, after pursuing her for months, she gave in and they began dating. They were popular in the neighborhood because they were both good-looking kids. My mom was smart and her smile could light up a room. My dad was dashing, could dance too and was the sharpest kid in the neighborhood. Sounds like the perfect couple, right? Wrong! Apparently, there was a lot of interference from others. Some were jealous of their relationship and some of his family members didn't approve of them dating.

The two of them had a strong connection and my mom fell in love and lost her virginity to my dad. Consequently, she was pregnant by the age of 16 at the beginning of her senior year of high school. Rumors circulated that he denied being the father. My mother was devastated and heartbroken. She was absolutely humiliated and everyone knew that he denied me. She broke up with him and decided to keep me with the support of my Grandmother. After giving birth to me she went back to school and graduated the following year.

So, as you can see they had a tumultuous history. It wasn't until a year later when his mom, my

Grandma Belle, saw me at the store that he accepted me. She said, "She is Wayne's baby." I obviously was the splitting image of my father. But for the first year of my life, I wasn't his…This history between them seem to fuel their relationship. Ultimately, affecting my relationship with my father. Time in my father's presence was limited. My mother never forgave him for abandoning us. A father is supposed to be a provider, protector; strong and powerful. My Grandmother became my father or at least she tried. Wayne, was my daddy.

I yearned for a daddy's love because I loved him intensely. My daddy made me feel special every time I saw him. I remember my dad buying me a pair of brown wooden shoes. I knew that *he* actually bought them because he was so proud when he gave them to me. He was so excited when he handed me the box. Normally my Grandparents, his parents, Grandma Belle and Granddaddy Daniel would buy me gifts for my birthday and Christmas. They were saved and in the church. But they weren't always saved.

My Grandma Belle spent many nights dragging my Granddaddy off the street corner. He was an alcoholic and would pass out regularly in front of the liquor store. My Granddaddy was what they called a functional alcoholic. He would go to the job every day, but once he was off, he would get drunk. Eventually he went into a program and got sober. He worked for Chrysler and there were programs designed to get you on track.

Grandma Belle received Christ first and eventually years later, my Granddaddy was saved. So anyway, my Grandparents would always send money and sign my dad's name to the card. That particular year, my dad personally gave me those shoes. I was eight years old. Those shoes were not the prettiest, but they were from my daddy, so I loved and cherished them. When my dad was in jail, my Grandparents would lie and say he was out of town working or on business. When he wasn't in jail he was in rehab. Oh, did I mention my father also had a drug addiction.

I found out later that he started using heroine at the age of 14. My Granddaddy discovered it when he bust open the bathroom door and found my father sitting on the toilet with a needle in his arm. This addiction plagued my dad for years and followed him into his adult life. My father was forever a child, it seems he never wanted to grow up. He was stuck in time and could not move past the seventies when his brother was a pimp.

Yes, my uncle was a real pimp. He even won Pimp of the Year, at the "The Twenty Grand" night club on 14th and Warren Ave. My Dad always wanted the fast money and the fast life. He didn't seem to grasp the reality that those days were over and that he had a little girl who needed him and wanted him to be a part of her life. He still lived in the past where they had mink coats, money and took trips to Vegas. The label of absentee father continued for many years. My father's rejection impacted my life in a way I could not have anticipated and I longed for his love.

A father's love is the first love, that a girl can experience and should experience, to set the standard in her life, of what love truly is! Unfortunately, I had nothing to gauge relationships. It's a father who teaches his daughter to be respected and valued by a man. He teaches her to be cherished and protected. A father is strong, provides and takes care of his family. A father is the instructor that sets the tone for all male relationships that will come later in life. He sets the bar and the rules.

When a young lady doesn't have a father in her life, there is an enormous void. My father's presence was missed in my life tremendously. Everything I had learned was one sided. For the most part, the only perspective I had, came from a woman's point of view. My only reference on relationships was based upon what I viewed as a child. I witnessed at times; volatile and abusive relationships. I saw physical and emotional abuse. I observed a lot of arguing, instead of real communication. I witnessed manipulation, blame, shame and overall…bitterness.

I guess by now you're thinking, Wow!!! Don't get me wrong, my childhood wasn't entirely bad. I did have some moments that truly shaped me positively. I have always been friendly, therefore I made friends rather easily. Some of my closest friends are from my childhood. Relationships from 2nd and third grade are prevalent in my life today. Kia and Kelly are friends that I met at a very young age. I met Kia when I was four years old. She lived down the street from me on Dexter.

Kia had everything! Bikes, dolls, and even a piano in her home. She was the baby girl in her family. Her family was middle-class and worked very hard. As a child, I thought they were rich. She was very giving and shared her toys. She was my friend.

Kelly lived on Dexter too. She and I connected while doing splits on the playground of Brady Elementary. She was a dancer. I remember her in her tutu playing the ballerina in the school plays. She and I became instant friends because I loved to dance too. Everyone didn't like me though. There were some who were mean to me and often teased me. I was very smart, but I didn't have the latest fashions or the 'flyest' hairstyles.

Let's be real. My mom wasn't a stylist. I remember the little pony tails that she would put in my hair and the pom-pom rubber bands. She tried her best, but it wasn't always good. My Aunt Allene would try to step in and help. She had this signature corn roll beehive hairstyle that she would give me. Let's just say that this hair-do increased the teasing. I appreciated her efforts though.

Not that my mother wasn't a good mom. Not at all…I remember her working with me day in and day out on spelling words for the Brady Elementary 5th grade spelling bee. I was so tired of her drilling me every day, but she was relentless. The day of the Bee, I could see her in the audience. I was so nervous, but all that hard work paid off. I won first place in the 5th Grade spelling Bee that year. I was ecstatic and she was so proud of me. There were moments like that, that would stay with me for a lifetime.

She made sure that I went to school and did my homework, but she was not always focused on me. She was young and had insecurities of her own. She had relationship issues with men who used her and cheated on her. Therefore, she wasn't emotionally stable at times or emotionally available for me. She did the best that she could under those circumstances. We had some good times. There were some happy moments between the women in my family and their love interests.

I was a flower girl in my Aunt Bunnie's wedding. She got married and walked down the aisle to the song "Forever Mine" by the O' Jays. The wedding was in our house on Dexter. It was a Christmas wedding with red beautiful poinsettia's everywhere. Mama went to the Eastern Market and had the living room decorated so beautifully. The fireplace was lit and Bunnie walked downed the aisle looking so pretty.

The house on Dexter Blvd was a two-family flat, and it was huge. We lived in the downstairs flat. It was a corner house with beautiful green vines on the outside. There were beautiful rose bushes and tulips that bloomed every year faithfully. The house had a huge porch with blue and white chairs. There was a huge living room with a fireplace, dining room and three bedrooms. We all lived in this house. My Grandmother, my two aunts, my uncle, mom and their children. Also, at some point and time they all lived there with their husbands. This was bittersweet at times.

I'm not saying this is true for all African American families, but for some, everyone living under one roof is not recommended. Especially when there are four women living together. There were times when everyone would get along. I remember hearing laughter, and music playing, the smell of greens and barbeque chicken in the kitchen, and my Mama's famous spaghetti with hamburger and sausage, topped with sharp cheddar cheese. Oh, and the cakes.... Chocolate, coconut, lemon and strawberry cakes. There was always baking and cooking going on in the house. Mmm mmm good. Mama was the best cook.

Grandma was the chief chef. She really could throw down in the kitchen. This made all her daughters great cooks. Every holiday was celebrated, but Mother's Day was their favorite! The ladies in my family would put on those pretty dresses and wear their beautiful corsages and take pictures in front of the house. It was a tradition for the ladies in our family. To get together and celebrate every holiday.

Sometimes we would all get invited to my Great Aunt Gwen's house. Gwen was my Grandmother's sister. She could also throw down in the kitchen. Gwen would have a feast: Barbeque ribs, chicken, collard greens and her famous macaroni and cheese. She was always having parties and inviting us over. Gwen was a giver and she had a heart of gold. I loved to go over her house and spend the night with my cousins. Those were some of the best times that I remember as a child. My Aunt Gwen's house was a home away from home for me. Sometimes I didn't want to go home. I guess it was because my cousins and I were around the same age.

Where I lived, I was the only girl so sometimes it was lonely. I was still the oldest and the boss though. Boys are boys, they were always playing and wrestling. I didn't care for dolls that much. I had a 'Baby-Dada Way Doll' that my Uncle John bought me. We had a special relationship. I suppose because

I was the first baby of the siblings. He took me to go see the movie The Wiz with Diana Ross and Michael Jackson. We rode the Dexter bus to the Adams Theater in downtown Detroit. My Uncle John always played jokes on me and this particular joke, I can recall vividly. I had a plastic inflatable Mickey Mouse. It wasn't very big, but it was big enough to be noticed. So anyway, one day my uncle called out for me. MiKi!!! Come here. I ran into the living room, but no one was there. Suddenly, I hear this voice. "Hey Miki, it's me Mickey!" The voice sounds like Mickey Mouse, but it's coming from the fireplace. I slowly turn and look. The plastic blow-up Mickey Mouse is sitting inside the fireplace. AHHHHHHHHH. I'm screaming, running and crying. My uncle starts to laugh. "It's just me my niece." He said in a sinister voice. He was hiding behind the chair in the living room.

Those times were crazy. We were always teasing and playing jokes on each other. There were a lot of good times growing up, but there were some miserable times too. Arguing, cussing and even fighting. I saw it all as a child. I believed with all my heart everyone loved each other. I just believe it was time to move on and no one really knew how to do it. I believed it was a fear especially for my mother. I remember an incident that occurred when I was a child that was extremely scary.

There was a couple that lived upstairs. The lady Cherrie was extremely jealous. She and her boyfriend would hang out downstairs sometimes with my family. Playing cards, drinking and partying. She thought that her boyfriend had a crush on my mom and she became very volatile. My mom was very pretty. She was petite with thick natural hair and had a nice shape. She was naturally beautiful and had a smile that would light up any room. I guess Kenny talked about her a little bit too much and Cherrie was furious.

One day she came on the downstairs porch talking trash about my mom. Well, my mom didn't believe in too much talking. She was a fighter. She would fight anybody. Men, women, it didn't matter. Even when my uncle would get into fights she would jump in when they were children. She believed in protecting her family, especially her brother and sisters. She did not care. So, when Cherrie began to talk, my Mom laughed at her and said. "Girl don't nobody want your man." Cherrie kept on talking and my Mom kept on laughing at her. My Aunt Allene who was pregnant at the time, tried to speak up and Cherrie threatened her. All hell broke loose then.

All I remember was Allene being pushed in the house by my Grandmother, Allene's husband and my Mom. Next thing you know, there were fists flying, pushing, shoving and Cherrie ran upstairs. About an hour later, two carloads full of people got out. Cherrie had called her family. My Grandmother called our family. We have a very huge family and a whole lot of friends. Eastside, Westside and North end all came with their guns. It was a big feud on Dexter and Hazelwood that day and I was really scared.

A guy tried to come in through our veranda on the side of our house. My uncle Vey pulled a sawed-off shotgun on him and told him to back up. He raised his hands talking about, he wasn't going to do anything. The feud intensified into the night and the police was called by Cherrie. I remember my Grandmother instructing me to keep the smaller children in the room. I didn't know what to think. I just obeyed her orders. I tried to keep everyone calm with games and snacks, but I was really petrified.

My family was sitting on the porch and the police told them to go in the house. My Grandmother asked why they had to go in the house, considering it was our porch. She stated that Cherrie had a porch upstairs that she and her family could sit on their porch upstairs. The police officer repeated that they had to go in to keep down confusion. As my Grandmother proceeded to walk in the house. Cherrie kicked her on the ankle. "Did you see her kick me?" My Grandmother asked. The officer of course did not see Cherrie kick her.

My Grandma came in the house and put on a big pot of water. The water begins to boil. We knew when my Grandmother got that big steel pot that it was going to be trouble. After about ten minutes and the water was boiling hot. She came to the front door. Cherrie and her family were still on the downstairs porch. My Grandma told the officer to move out of the way. She yelled some obscenities before trying to scald Cherrie. The police officer yelled. "Don't do it!" Grandma threw the pot of boiling water. The police officer screamed. "Damn, she got me too." Grandma was arrested that night. Thank God, the officer did jump back, but yes some of the water did reach Cherrie. She wasn't severely burned or anything, but the act itself was a crime.

I saw my Grandma arrested that night. My mother tried to remain calm, but she was upset. We all were traumatized. She was charged with felonious assault. That was a long night. The next day my Aunt Bunnie was arrested too because she went ballistic hearing that her mother was in jail.

The officers yelled at the precinct, "We have another Calhoun." My Grandma knew it was Bunnie. They were saying that it was a mini riot on Dexter and Hazelwood. Cherrie threw a brick through our living room window after Grandma went to jail. My mother had to use wisdom about retaliation because we were there. My Aunt Bunnie then threw a brick through their upstairs front window, again in front of the police and that's how she got arrested. After a couple of days Grandma was released. Cherrie moved about a week later.

Grandma and Mama had a sawed-off shotgun and were sitting in the living room waiting for them to start something before they left. They had already broken our front room window during the feuding. They assumed the night of the move there was going to be drama. I had to keep the children in the room once again. I did peek out and saw them leaning up against the window with the shotgun.

I guess Cherrie and her gang were too tired to leave with a bang. They left peacefully. Grandma had been charged and had to go to court. The fact that she had a job and worked for so many years worked in her favor. She eventually received probation and had to do community service. Those were some crazy and dangerous times.

Well, in between the fights, feuds and chaos; marriages were forming and also falling apart. After marrying and professing their love and devotion to each other, my Aunt Bunnie and her husband were fussing, fighting and ultimately splitting up. Most of the marriages I witnessed as a child and teenager were not good marriages. My Grandparents met in Black Bottom when she was 15 years old. Black Bottom is an area in Detroit that has great history. There was an enormous amount of black-owned businesses that flourished in that community. Such as dentist offices, cleaners, Jazz-clubs, restaurants, bakeries, you name it.

Though my Grandmother and Grandfather were still married, they had been separated for almost 30 years. My Grandmother married my Grandfather at the age of 17. They fell in love and she was trying to leave home and her evil step mother. Her step-mother didn't want her there either, so she signed for them to get married. My Grandfather abused my Grandmother, which made her very bitter toward him. She stayed with him for 8 years, had 4 children and then finally decided to leave, when she felt he was about to kill her.

It took strength and courage to walk away in those days. Most women would stay because they wouldn't have anywhere else to go. Women married young in the 40's and 50's. My Grandfather was the provider of the family and she had 4 children in succession to a man that had a drug addiction. When she met him, he was not addicted to drugs. He worked and they got along great. He didn't even smoke marijuana, but as the years progressed she began to see a change in him. Seems his drug of choice was heroin. I'm convinced that drugs are from Satan. They come to destroy lives and families. You destroy the man, you destroy the family unit.

I never understood why they didn't just divorce? After years of estrangement, he began to come around again. Fortunately, my Grandfather was rehabilitated from drugs, became a Jehovah's Witness and turned his life around. On Christmas, Thanksgiving and sometimes weekends, he would bring fruit from the Eastern Market. He wouldn't say anything crazy, he knew he would be escorted out with a quickness.

I remember one incident. I will never forget it. He changed his life and I thank God for that. During this time, he was spreading the word of Jehovah and wouldn't drink or indulge in any kind of drugs. He was redeemed and living for God. So, this particular Christmas, he was at the house and we were talking about Santa. I was so excited. "Daddy John, I can't wait for Santa to come, I have been so good this year." He replied, "What are you talking about? There is no Santa." The music was loud, we always had the record player on and we had all the jams. The O'Jays, The Temptations, Smokey Robinson and the Miracles. My family loved music. All I remember was "What the hell did you say to her?" The music was abruptly cut off. "Get the hell out!" Daddy John was cursed out by my Mama.

My Mama had issues with her dad and their relationship was strained. You see, she was the oldest of the four children. Therefore, she saw and heard a great deal during those eight years she lived in the home with him and my grandmother. She witnessed some of the abuse and had to step in and assist with her siblings. She was made to grow up pretty fast. It was shameful and sad, but he had to go! There was no explaining. There was no discussion. It was cut and dry. This is the foundation that I had to build on. This is how love was viewed in my eyes growing up, with all that confusion as my foundation. I found myself always searching and seeking love from daddy which eventually transferred into a yearning for any kind of love or affection from men.

Love Nots

Daddy's Love

1.

Evil Knocked, She Answered

My mother met my Stepfather Charles in 1980. The day she met him, our lives changed. My Grandmother never liked him. She felt that he was sneaky and a con artist. Quiet as it was kept, I didn't like him either. I knew there was something about him that was fraudulent. After a short courtship, he managed to slither his way into our lives and with him, came a multitude of problems. I guess you're wondering how and why did she even marry him. Well, he was the king of deception. He was charismatic, well dressed, poised and very articulate. Charles was a reverend, an accountant and anything you name, he was. He was the ultimate con artist. He even worked in a law office, wore a suit and tie every day and carried a brief case.

My mother really believed that after having her heart broken by my dad first, then my brother's dad, that this man, was the man of her dreams. He hid the

27

fact that he had a drug addiction until after they were married. He was such a con, that he was even able to get himself written in the book of Who's Who in America. His mother revealed years later that he was bitten by a snake as a child down south and that he almost died. He *was* a snake! A liar, thief and he deceived my mother, who had unresolved issues with her own father. Can you see the pattern? Well, after they were married and he moved in, all hell broke loose in our family. He quit his job and just became dominating and useless. I imagine his pattern was to work long enough until he found a woman he could sucker into taking care of him.

When I started Halley Middle School, she would have him walk me to school. Maybe she thought this would allow us to bond. He would talk to me and ask me questions. It irritated the heck out of me. I would walk silently all the way to Brady. That was the pickup and drop off for the bus. I just didn't understand why she allowed this low-life to enter our lives. She simply loved him. I believe she wanted to save him. She saw the potential in him and didn't want to abandon him. It seems that women have a natural proclivity to see the potential in a man and think they can help him become something more than what he is today. But the truth is, if he can't see his own potential and want to become more, potential is all they'll ever have.

Charles was extremely intelligent, but he had another side. Charles was a real-life Dr. Jekyll and Mr. Hyde. Mom was smitten by him because he would sweet talk her and make her laugh. There *were* times I saw them happy, but not often. I watched her become more and more isolated from her friends. Even though some of her friends were bad influences and she needed to not see them.

One time I saw her and her friend Brenda doing cocaine. I peeped through the key hole in her bedroom door. She had a tiny straw and there was powder on an album cover and she snorted it. I never said anything to her, but I did see it. I don't believe she did it regularly, but I believe it was an outlet for a life that was already chaotic. Mama was a dreamer and wanted a good life. She just didn't know how to acquire that life. Charles talked the dreamer talk and filled her head with all kinds of promises. He knew that she desired a home of her own. He would dangle that like a carrot. He hated the bond that mama had with Grandma. He even shouted that he hated her during a heated argument. "I hate your mother," he told my mother. My Grandmother heard him and responded. "So, you hate me, but continue to eat my cooking. I could poison you." "Keep on hating me." He was so upset he turned blue.

Charles was always up late cleaning and mopping the floors around the house. I believe he thought he could con my Grandmother by cleaning all the time. My Grandmother was a professional cleaner, why would she need him to clean her house? I often wondered as a child, why he was up at 2 a.m. mopping floors. He was a night owl and would come in faithfully about 10 p.m. every night with a pint of Haagen-Dazs vanilla ice-cream, Archway oatmeal cookies and Welches Grape juice. Our mouths would be salivating with anticipation waiting for the snacks. He wouldn't offer us a crumb. Nothing! I would be so upset. We were children and we wanted the sweets and goodies. He was so stingy and selfish to us.

My mother would ask him why would he bring the bags in and not offer us anything. This was a frequent argument. Sometimes he would give in and other times he was relentless about not sharing. My brother didn't like him either. Charles wanted to beat him and my mother would stop him. Although, my brother was a bit temperamental and disobedient at times. He didn't deserve to be beaten. A good spanking every now and again, but never beaten. My Stepfather was extremely jealous of my mother's relationship with my brother. They had a bond. I guess because she absolutely loved his father. You see, we all had different fathers. I believed that had an effect on our relationships. I love my brothers, but there was a slight disconnect. Although, they're my blood, it's not full blood. It's not blood in blood out and ultimately this had a slight affect with our closeness.

I'm not sure if this topic is discussed or even acknowledged, but this is just my opinion on the subject manner. I'm not trying to disgrace my mother in any way. These are just facts. We did have three different fathers and that was because my mom was searching for this wonderful fulfilling love, that she never received. She failed over and over again, but as a result, brought children into this world. Well, as I stated earlier, Charles came with a multitude of problems.

One summer night, after my brother was born, we were all sleeping in the living room because it was immensely hot that night. My mom and Charles were in the back room with my baby brother. All of a sudden, we heard all of these gun shots. POW POW POW!!! Then the glass shattered. Someone shot through the back of our house and threw a Molotov cocktail through the upstairs flat. Everyone was screaming and hollering. My mom grabbed my brother and hit the floor.

We were all terrified. Fortunately, the floor was concrete in the upstairs flat's back room. So no one was hurt. God was with us that night. After, the police arrived; we were informed there was another cocktail in the alley. The cops assumed it was for the downstairs, which was our house. The streets were talking and we heard that Charles owed someone some dope money and that's why we were targeted. Of course, he denied it. That was the first time we heard that he had an addiction. It was hard to prove it because we lived in a 2-family flat with an entire different family upstairs.

His argument was, it could have been directed to someone in the upper flat. My grandmother warned my mother, told her to leave him and to protect her children. My mom argued with her and believed her husband. No one could say anything bad about him without her defending him. This man didn't work, didn't bring home any money and began to slowly degrade my mother and abuse her emotionally and physically. I hated him. I knew he wasn't right.

As time passed, I was losing respect for my mother for staying with him. I started disrespecting her more and more. Talking back and she would pop me in my mouth. In 1984 our house caught on fire. I remember waking up to glass breaking. My Grandmother and I shared a room. I heard the glass, then I smelled the smoke. We could hear screaming from my Aunt Bunnie who lived next door. THE HOUSE IS ON FIRE! My Grandma screamed for everyone to get out. The fire started in the upstairs flat. Our neighbor Karen and her daughter were home. Her daughter was an adult that had special needs, but was functional. She was hit by a car on Livernois Ave and suffered some brain damaged and dragged her foot when she walked. Ciara lost her earring in the bed and used a lighter to try and find it. The mattress caught on fire and they poured water on the mattress. They thought the fire was out. The mattress was still burning inside and the house caught on fire. Their bedroom was above ours. Hence, hearing the window glass breaking.

By the time the Fire Department came, the house was destroyed. This was March 17, 1984. The Firemen pulled Karen and her daughter out and laid them on the grass. I still remember seeing the frost on the grass with their bodies lying there. They had smoke inhalation and had to go to the hospital. Thank God, they survived. Their dog died though. It was a Doberman Pinscher. Our house downstairs was not burned, but the water damage destroyed everything. It was unlivable. I stayed out of school for about two weeks.

My mom received vouchers from the Red Cross and the State of Michigan. We received vouchers for clothes and appliances. My Step-father took the washer and dryer that was purchased with the voucher and sold them. In our time of distress, he was still conniving and scamming with his criminal acts. During this time, I was at Halley Middle school and I was miserable. Those were some of the worst years of my childhood. I suffered emotionally and mentally, plus my grades suffered horribly. I had gone from being a straight A student at Brady Elementary school to getting C's and D's in Halley middle school. Not to mention, I was bullied for years there, because of my hair and clothes.

We were considered poor, low-income and didn't have a lot. The one thing I did have going on for me was my ability to dance. I could dance, so I became popular in middle school for that. I could always pull a circle around me dancing at the annual school dances. Dancing has always been my outlet. It has always brought me joy and peace even through all the misery. After the fire, we moved in with my Aunt Bunnie. Actually, it was for the best because my cousins were home alone a great deal.

My Aunt had started using heroin and would disappear for days at a time. The family was so hurt and distraught that she had become addicted to drugs. Especially because of the history of my Grandfather and his addiction. Sometimes my mother and grandma would hit the pavement looking and searching for my Aunt. She used to hang in the area near the Dexter Car Wash on Dexter. There was

33

a lot of drug traffic in that neighborhood. My Grandma worried about her daughter, but she had to put the children first. She eventually had to get guardianship and my Mom stepped in to help raise my little cousins with no hesitation!

My Grandmother was working for the Board of Education as a custodian. She would walk to work every day. I respect her so much because she took the job that no one wanted and held that job with integrity and honor. She went to work every day and never missed a beat. She had over 200 sick days when she retired 30 years later. She took care of her family and held that job with pride. She was the head of our household. She worked and provided for us all. There were some hard times, but the love never stopped. There were times we went without lights and even gas. I remember waking up for school sometimes by the sun because there was no electricity for an alarm clock. There were also times we sat by candlelight and just talked. We tried not to let the tough times get to us. She encouraged her children to work. They would work odd jobs. I remember my mother working for Hudson's department store, but it was just for Christmas.

My Aunt worked for Queen Quality cleaners for a while and my Uncle John worked for Churches Chicken for about two weeks and quit. She was the only adult with stable employment. I guess that's why she had all the control and all the power. She paid the cost to be the boss. It was obvious though that she couldn't do it all. That's why we had those tough times, but we always had each other. My

Grandmother had endured some hardships, but she never gave up. I have so much admiration for her as a woman and as a person. She always put her family first and took care of everyone.

Shortly after the fire, Charles went to jail. He was prosecuted for writing bad checks and would send letters from jail every week. I was happy that he went to jail. I felt like I had my Mom back. She started hanging with her friends again and having fun. She surprised me and took me to go see Prince's movie "Purple Rain." We took the Grand River bus to the Norwest Theater and had a wonderful time. She didn't tell me where we were going. When I saw that marquee, I just started screaming. I was sooooo happy. This was a moment that was ours. It was just the two of us. We laughed and cried and really enjoyed the movie. Our relationship was beginning to shift. I was growing up and was becoming that awkward teenager. I was between a girl and a woman, and boy did I have a mouth. I had inherited that mouth. Lord have mercy! Sometimes that mouth got me in a lot of trouble. My mother had to check me often about my sarcasm and attitude.

I got my first job through the summer youth program. The summer youth program was for children from low-income families between the ages of 14 and 18. These programs were created to give children something to do for the summer by giving them an opportunity to work in the city. That was my very first job. I was 14 years old and placed at Winter Halter Middle school picking up paper and keeping the grounds clean. I made 70.00 a week and I was 'geeked'. I bought my first silver chain and bracelet to match. I was finally able to buy clothes and gym shoes.

My mother would buy me pumpkin seed gym shoes from Woolworth and Pro-Wings from Payless on Dexter Ave. I hated those shoes. I bought myself a pair of satin blue EBS gym shoes. My friends Kia and Shellie had those shoes and I asked Mama to buy me a pair. Listen, she bought me a pair of burgundy corduroy EBS. I was appalled! I was wearing corduroy gym shoes in the summertime. So, I most definitely had to get the satin ones with my check. I also helped with some of the bills.

The following year I was 15 and worked for the Kim Westin Festival of the Performing Arts Summer Youth program. Kim Westin was with Motown Records and she recorded the song "It Take Two" with the late Marvin Gaye. She had a grant and created this awesome way to expose children to the Arts. There were classes that taught music, photography, acting, audio visual and of course my passion, Dance. I was paid to take dance classes. Now that's a cool job! I took African dance with the legend Ali Abdullah, who I auditioned for years later in 1990, when Nelson Mandela came to Detroit.

I performed with him and other dancers at Tiger Stadium. That was truly an honor. Okay, back to the summer program. The classes also consisted of Ballet and Modern Dance with the legendary Clifford Fears and many other talented dance teachers. Every year at the end of the summer we gave a performance at Hart Plaza. So this was a wonderful experience for me to learn stage production, dance technique and receive training by the best in the city of Detroit.

As I got older my mom was beginning to get frustrated with me. She was upset because I made her accountable for her decisions. I believed that she was 90% responsible for our situation. There wasn't any stability and things were always uncertain. As a child, I worried a great deal. Children are not supposed to worry about adult issues. She avoided conversations with me because I challenged her. She favored my two brothers and she absolutely adored them. Especially my middle brother. He could do no wrong in her eyes. My youngest brother was simply her baby. That speaks volumes. She loved him so much. There was some happiness and joy in the family again. Although, we still *struggled*, the love never stopped. We were a family. We had once again moved and were living on Dexter and Atkinson, in a 4-family flat. My mother lived upstairs and Grandma lived downstairs. I would travel between both flats, but I mainly lived downstairs with Grandma. It was there that I met my first love.

Love Nots

Evil Knocked, She Answered

2.

First Love

I had a crush on a very nice boy. I was sweet 16 and had never been kissed. Well… Not a real kiss anyway. The boy sneaking a kiss and then running off doesn't count, nor does a kiss during spin the bottle. I saw him in Thrifty Scot grocery store on Joy road. He was a stock boy there. He looked Indian and had pretty caramel skin and gorgeous hair. He was sort of quiet though, but he *was* sweet. I was attracted to his demeanor and the fact that he was easy on the eyes was a bonus. One day I was sitting on the porch of my house, bored as ever, he walked by woofing down a Coney dog. A. Eagles Coney Island was on the corner of Joy road and Dexter and they made the best Coney's in Detroit. Anyway, because I was bored, I decided to pick with him. "Wow, slow down you must be really hungry?" He was embarrassed. He didn't even see me sitting on the porch. He blushed and didn't say a word. About a week later, I saw him in the hall at Central High school. I couldn't believe my eyes, he was standing at the locker so I approached him and then grabbed his notebook to find out his name. James…. hmmm. He told me that he was a senior and was about to graduate. This was the last week of May in 1986. That Friday, Memorial Day weekend, I looked his name up in the White Pages. I remember that he told me that he was a junior and there was his father's name in black and white. I had my friend Kia call him and pretend to be me. She was more mature. She had a boyfriend already and was comfortable with talking to boys on the phone. She called and pretended to be me.

I was there with her when she made the call. We were two silly teenage girls having fun. They stayed on the phone for about 15 minutes, as I sat there listening and hanging on to his every word. She gave him my number and he called that night and spoke to *me*. James and I began dating and I fell for him hard. He grew up so different from me. He had a two-parent home and his siblings were older and already established. I really admired that. His Father worked a full-time job and his mom was a housewife.

James was the artistic type - he could draw. He loved sports and jazz. He wasn't a thug either. He came from a foundation that I just couldn't relate to, because my Grandmother was the head of our household. His household was quite the contrary to mine. But that didn't stop us from talking on the phone every night. He was a true gentleman. He never tried to kiss me or touch me inappropriately.

My mom knew that I liked him. She warned me about being fast and boys. One day I slept to noon and she went ballistic. She came into my room yelling and screaming and accusing me of being pregnant. She told me to get dressed because we were going to the Doctor. I tried to convince her that I wasn't pregnant, but she didn't believe me. I told her that I was not having sex and was still a virgin. She didn't believe that either. So, we walked around to the clinic on Joy road. It was a storefront walk in clinic. As we waited for the doctor. I tried to explain to her that she was mistaken and that I was still a virgin. She was not hearing it!

Finally, the physician entered and began to talk to us. He asked a series of questions regarding my age? Whether I had a boyfriend or not? Finally, he examined me. He assured my mother that I was still a virgin, but suggested that she put me on birth control because I did have a boyfriend. He prescribed Ortho-Novum 7-7-7 28. They were little multicolored pills, which I had to take every day. My life would never be the same. Once the approval of sex is initiated, it opens the door to committing the act. Though our relationship was still in the beginning stage, the pill, made sex, a very possible option…permission to have sex if you will. It is important to guard our young women. Wait until you get married is not preached enough in our culture. I opened myself up to emotions of rage, jealousy, insecurity and a whole lot of other feelings. We were together for 2 years.

Our courtship was really innocent in the beginning. He took me to Red Lobster on Sweetest day. I had never been there before. It was after homecoming. I was a member of my high school dance company and we marched in the parade that day. So it was a nice ending to a fantastic day. He suggested that I order the lobster. He knew I had never tasted it. I also ordered the crab legs, but was disgusted by the taste. He taught me how to play pool, introduced me to the jazz singer, Michael Frank's "Popsicle Toes" and The Tigers. He loved baseball games at Tiger Stadium on Trumbull. Those were the best hotdogs I have ever tasted. I had never been to a baseball game. It was exciting and James wanted to expose me to cultural things. He wanted to broaden my horizons.

He was particularly attracted to my mind. He loved the fact that I was an Honor student and that I loved to dance. I was a member of the Central Dance Company under the direction of Mrs. Lumpkin. He supported me in The Detroit Public Schools, All-City Dance concerts, talent shows and he encouraged me to go to college and have a career. He was a true gentleman and in my eyes my knight and shining armor. I just knew that I would marry James one day. He was my first love. I lied to James and told him I wasn't a virgin. Why I felt the need to lie, I don't know? Most girls are proud to say they are a virgin, but for some reason. I was not.

During that time, my friends had already lost their virginity and I had not. I felt left out for some reason. They would sit and talk about their experiences and

I would feel so immature. I wanted to feel that closeness with someone. I wanted to feel loved. I felt a need to grow up really fast and had no idea why…or what I was doing. Our conversations started to lean more and more toward sex. I knew eventually it was going to happen. Although, I was an honor student, I skipped one day and met him at his brother's house. He went to the store and bought the condoms. He was adamant about not becoming a father. We tried, but it didn't happen. I felt awful and blamed myself. I must be doing something wrong I thought. He was very quiet, which I didn't understand and it made me feel really insecure. A couple of days later, there was a weird awkwardness in our relationship. Finally, I realized I had to tell him the truth. He came to visit me one night and as we sat on the stairs in the inside of our flat. I admitted to him that I was a virgin. I was too afraid to tell him directly. So, I wrote it on a brown paper bag. He read the note stood up, kissed me on the cheek and left.

I was horrified. All kind of thoughts ran through my mind. "Oh my God he is going to leave me". I panicked and took off running down the street. Suddenly, I could hear my mom yelling Miki!!!!! I didn't look back. I ran all the way to my friend Shellie's house. I proceeded to tell her what happened. She laughed at me of course and asked, "Why did you lie?" I replied, "I don't know." Next thing I know James was standing on the sidewalk. "What are you doing here?" I asked. He told me that he heard my Mom screaming my name. He told me to go home and he would call me. He told me that he was not upset and would call me in an hour. He explained that he wanted to talk to me. I waited patiently.

Finally, I went home and waited for his call. James confessed to me that he was relieved after reading my note. He was relieved because he was a virgin too. I was so happy. This news just confirmed in my mind that we were meant to be together. That explained why we failed the time we tried. Neither one of us knew what we were doing. Unbelievable! It happened spontaneous one summer night at his house. His mom was out of town and his dad was asleep. I had no idea what I was doing, I didn't feel any different. I just knew that things would never be the same.

I equated sex with love. I had no idea what real love was. James and I were inseparable. My mom really didn't care for him. She thought that we were way too young to be that serious and was afraid that I would end up hurt. James wanted an education and he came from a family of educators. He had a fear of me becoming pregnant. That was his biggest fear and that was also my mom's biggest fear. My mother wanted me to go to school and get a degree. She wanted me to accomplish all the things that she didn't have a chance to. She was so hard on me pertaining to matters of the heart. I did understand her paranoia, but James wasn't like the men I witnessed growing up. Although, he was not like those men, I was still damaged by the things that I saw.

Those bad habits and behaviors slowly began to manifest in my relationship. The blooming romance began to sour. Believe me, it was not him. I almost thought it was boring to not have an argument or a disagreement. So, I would look for ways to be upset. I was modeling what I believed how women behaved in relationships. The break up to make up syndrome. So we argued a lot and he wasn't the arguing type. His family was peaceful. I couldn't even call his house after 10.00 p.m., because his parents were in bed asleep. In my household people were up all-night long. Now don't get me wrong, my family wasn't bad. It was just my household did not consist of a two-parent home. There was some dysfunction, but we loved each other.

Ultimately, something that was pure and beautiful, I destroyed. I can admit that now. I never had a real male figure in my life. I didn't know how to respect him or treat him. The day that James broke up with me, I can remember it so vividly. He was diagnosed with diabetes. James was beginning to drink a lot of water, pop, you name it. Eventually he had to go to the hospital and he received the diagnosis. His whole life changed. No more drama from me. He had to make a decision to take care of his body and stay stress free. He broke up with me that day in the hospital. I cried and begged him to give me another chance. He told me that he loved me, but that he could no longer be in a relationship. He had to remain healthy and stress free.

I was a freshman in college during this time. He told me that I should focus on school and that we could remain friends. I was heartbroken. I remember going home and crying myself to sleep. I just didn't understand why he ended things. I said horrible things to him in retaliation of him breaking my heart. I was hurt, but I didn't allow him to see my pain. Instead I attacked him verbally. I did what was normal to me. What I grew up seeing. The women in my family were not weak and I was taught to never allow a man to get the best of me. To always use my mouth as a weapon.

Although, I was hurt and missed him terribly, I never allowed myself to be vulnerable for too long. The minute he rejected my pleas to reconcile, I would literally curse him out. That's what the women in my family did. I witnessed this behavior as a child and teenager my entire life. The husbands and boyfriends got cussed out. I adapted to that behavior. It became a shield, a defense mechanism. My mouth became my weapon as I got older.

Charles was let out of prison for good behavior. He came back into our lives and I was disgusted once again. I had noticed some changes with my mother. She was hanging with her friends more and she wanted to have long heart felt conversations with me. I really wasn't interested in them. I was young and had my friends and didn't want the burdens any longer of my Mom and Step-father.

I had auditioned for a scholarship, "A Talent Award" in Dance. I was truly into the Arts. I loved to dance. I feel freedom when I dance and it was the only time I felt truly happy. I had never taken a technical dance class until I attended Central High

School under the instruction of Ms. Lumpkin. She saw my potential and began to challenge and help me develop artistically. God gave me a gift and I was so excited about the audition. I arrived and I was the only black girl. I immediately became intimidated and felt inferior to those girls. They were there in their tutu's and ballet shoes. I didn't have any fancy costume. As a matter of fact, I had my white Unitard with the feet out. As I watched them stretch, laugh and giggle amongst one another, I started to feel I didn't belong there. So I left the dance room and went to the pay phone. I called my mother and told her what and how I was feeling. She said, "Well if you think they are better than you, then just get on the bus and come home." I responded. "Mom I never said they were better than me!" She proceeded. "Well you're complaining and talking about how good they are, just come home then!" She then hung up the phone. I stared at the phone in utter disbelief. I know now that she was using reverse psychology on me. That tough love. She always used that tough love on me. It made me strong!!! It made me resilient!!! It made me prove her wrong. I was not intimidated by those girls and yes, I was just as good as they were.

I went in that audition and I gave it everything!!!! They were clapping for me by the time I was done with my audition piece. I will never forget that moment. The Director of the Dance Department, Georgia Reid called my Mom and told her how wonderful I was and that she was so proud and impressed. I received the Talent scholarship. I was so happy!

3.

Mommy's Death

After 7 years of marriage, she was finally fed up with him and his lifestyle and had separated from him in the summer of 1988. As a matter of fact, that's the summer I graduated from high school with honors. I had already been inducted into the National Honor Society and would be the first in our immediate family to attend a major university. I was accepted to Wayne State University and she was extremely happy and proud of me. I had also auditioned and was accepted to Alvin Ailey Intensive Dance program for the following summer.

My life was changing for the better and I had a wonderful and bright future. Six months after witnessing her oldest child, her only daughter graduate from high school, she was gone. Due to the contraction of AIDs, Acquired Immune Deficiency Syndrome, my mom died January 21, 1989. She was 36 years old. I was 18 years old at the time. The disease was passed to her through her husband. My mother had a cold for about two weeks and barely had the strength to leave the couch. She was so weak and didn't have any energy. She was taking cough medicines and home remedies and nothing was changing. I remember my Grandmother and me begging her to go to the hospital. Finally, she did! It was on a Friday night and I was working the midnight shift at Mobil. The gas station was directly across the street from our house. She came to the window and told me that she was going to the hospital. I was so happy. I encouraged her and told her that was the best news that I'd heard all day. She smiled and waved.

My mother Laura went to the hospital for treatment of a cold and within a week was dead. She never came home. It was there that she was diagnosed with the disease and in the last stages of the illness. There was nothing the doctors could do for her at that point. My Step-father had deceived her by convincing her that the medication prescribed for him was for his kidneys, but in fact he was taking the drug AZT for HIV to prolong his life. We discovered that he had been on this medication for years.

The day my mom died was the saddest day of my life. I caught the bus to Henry Ford Hospital from Wayne State. She had been admitted for about four days and the doctors were continuing to run tests to see what was causing her illness. First, they thought

Mommy's Death

she had tuberculosis. That was then ruled out. She was coughing and could barely breathe when I arrived at the hospital that Friday. I walked in the room, greeted her, kissed her on the forehead and proceeded to ask her the usual questions. I said, "How are you feeling Mama? She was very quiet and told me that she was fine. I felt something was wrong. I gave her a card that I had bought from the gift shop. She asked me about my classes and I pretended to be excited about my life as a freshman in college. I wasn't though, I was worried about my mom. I asked her what she wanted me to do with the card, if she wanted me to hang it on the wall. She began to get really frustrated with me. "Miki, I can't do everything for you, some things you're going to have to do for yourself. You're 18 now!" Ummm Okay?! I'll just hang it here. Again silence. A very long eerie silence.

"When the doctor comes in I want you to leave" Why do I have to leave Mama? Because I said so. Okay, I didn't argue with her, I didn't give her any lip. I asked her if she wanted any make up on, she responded yes. I applied foundation and put some pink lipstick on her lips. Pink was her favorite color. She was weak, frail, but I knew how much she loved to wear her make up. I thought it would bring her some happiness to at least looked pretty. My Grandmother and Aunt Allene arrived. She told me to leave the room. I didn't understand, but I obeyed anyone. I was gone for about 10 minutes. I knew something was terribly wrong. When I walked back in the room my Grandmother was holding my mom's foot. My Grandma told her that she would be fine, that she would take care of her and that she was going to cook her some mustard and turnip greens when she came home.

My mom nodded, but her foot wouldn't stop shaking. My Aunt was crying. I demanded for them to tell me what was going on. No one listened to me. "I'm 18 now please tell me what's wrong?" At this point tears are streaming down my face. NO one answered me. Finally, after a long pause we said our goodbyes and left the hospital. We took the Dexter bus home. That bus ride was the longest and most silent ride ever. When we arrived home, Grandma wanted to speak with my brother Mari and me. Since I was the oldest she directed everything to me. Laura has AIDS. All I remember was screaming and dropping to my knees crying. No God!!! No God!!! Crying… I knew what that meant I knew she was dying. AIDS was new on the scene, we really didn't know too much about the disease. Just that gay men were dying from it and that you could contract it from heterosexual sex and sharing dirty needles.

My Grandmother was numbed, but so strong. I never saw her break down. She hid that from us. She cried privately. My mother was her first-born child, she nursed her on her breast and I know she was broken. She held it together for us. My mom helped her raise my Aunt Bunnies' children. My Grandmother looked at my mother as her Rock. Grandma was the family's Rock, but my mother was Her Rock. After, getting my composure, I called my mama on the phone and she was so apologetic for a lot of things. She had so many regrets about allowing Charles in our lives and her use of cocaine. I told her that none of that mattered. I told her that I wanted to speak to her in person and put my arms around her and hug her. That evening grandma called all the family to the house to inform them of Mom's illness. The house was packed.

Everyone went back down to the hospital to see her. My mom told my grandma to not treat my Step-father any different. This was fine to her because she couldn't stand him anyway. So nothing changed. She also made her promise to never let him or his family take my baby brother. She wanted my grandmother to raise him. My Mom, I was told was extremely worried about me. She felt that I was "Green". She knew that I was naive and didn't want me to be taken advantage of by people. I decided to wait until the next day because I wanted to talk to her alone. I had so many things I wanted to say to her. I wanted to tell her Thank you for being so hard on me. I wanted to thank her for pushing me, to strive for excellence. I wanted to tell her that I LOVE HER. I wanted to tell her that I admired her for being a single mother and raising me to the best of her ability without a father. I wanted to tell her that I was proud of her for going back and finishing school.

I had all these things I wanted to say to her. Everyone went and saw her, but me. That night around 2:00 am in the morning. We received a call from the hospital to come immediately. When we arrived, they told us that my Mom was brain dead. Apparently, they found her on the floor. She had gone into cardiac arrest and there was no brain activity and she was on a ventilator. It was decided that we would let her go. My Grandmother didn't want my Mom to live like that. She had too much Zest for life, and was a free spirit. I went in and talked to her. Hoping she could hear me. I kissed her on her forehead and I told her that I love her. After she passed, a male nurse asked if he could speak with us. He told us that he was saved and that he had talked to my mom about Salvation. He told us that she had received Jesus Christ as her Lord and Savior that week. I really didn't know how powerful that was back then. No one in my family went to church.

My first-time attending was in the 5th grade. My teacher Mrs. Ducree invited a few of us to her church on Easter Sunday. I asked my Mom if I could go all week, but she never responded. Well, Sunday arrived and I was dressed in my yellow dress with the patent leather red shoes and a purse to match. We always dressed for Easter, my family would cook, play music and the children always had baskets and jelly beans, but we didn't go to church. The horn blows. "They're here, they're here. I ran across the bed with my shoes on. My Grandmother said. "What the hell is going on?" You don't run across the bed. Have you lost your mind? "But they're here." I repeated. "Who's here?" They both said simultaneously. I said, "Mama I told you that I was going to church today."

She responded again, "Girl what are you talking about?" She looks out the window and sees a van on the side of the house. My mama walks me to the minivan. There are about five children in the van with little greased faces. Everyone is excited to see me. "I thought you were making this up?" I'm going to let you go this time because all your friends are in the car. "My mom decides then to let me attend. I knew one prayer and that was Psalms 23. My Grandmother read it to me when I was 8 years old. She challenged me to memorize it after she read it. She gave me 20 minutes to memorize it, then recite it to her. Knowing Mom had received Christ gave the family some peace, but our lives were forever changed.

I couldn't stop crying and I was in a daze. I went to the hospital's pay phone and called James. I told him about Mama. He gave his condolences and we hung up the phone. We started to plan Mama's funeral. My mother back in June had taken out an insurance policy. I remember sitting on the couch and her discussing it with me. She had made me the beneficiary. She told me that if anything ever happened to her that she wanted me to get a real house. The insurance policy was for 10,000. I was angry with her. "What are you talking about?" Nothing is going to happen to you. "You never know." She replied. As I reflect back maybe she knew…. Well, we never got the insurance money.

During the planning of the funeral. The insurance company had to investigate because of her illness and the fact that the policy was less than 2 years old. They had to look into her medical history. Back then, she had Medicaid and identification wasn't required as much when using insurance. It was just a piece of blue paper. There were times when my Aunt Bunnie would have to go back and forth in the hospital suffering with her addiction. My aunt didn't have insurance, but my mom being the person she was gave her the insurance card to see about herself. So after the investigation, the report read that my mom was a heroin addict, so the insurance company didn't pay. Also, they said the policy was too new. So my Grandfather "Daddy John" wrote a check that day at James Cole Funeral Home.

My Grandma looked over and said, "There's her father right there." My mother was beautiful. Her favorite color was pink. She had on a beautiful pink chiffon dress. She also had a rose-colored casket. A friend of our family worked at Cole's so he assured us that she would be well taken care of. Everyone came, my friends and my teachers. My favorite teachers were there, my dance teacher Mrs. Lumpkin-Jones and English teacher Mr. Vincent Garrity. I cried when I saw them. I even cried and broke down at my mother's casket.

Grandma wasn't having that though. She told me to stop it and get it together. She reminded me to be strong and told someone to take me to the back. The sun was shining bright that day. God was letting us know that his daughter had arrived. My Uncle Jim was a deputy chief at the time and he made the arrangement for a police escort to the cemetery. That's when I knew there had to be more than just life on this earth. There must be a heaven. I remember thinking, for a person to be in your life, for you to love them and then, they're taken from you, there must be some explanation. There must be a heaven. If not, then all of this is a cruel joke.

In my mind. I needed my mother. I was underdeveloped and undernourished emotionally. I didn't know anything about love. I was just a freshman in college; very green and naïve when it came to the world. After my mother died, I knew God had to be real. For my mother to be here one day and then gone the next. That's when I wanted to know more about the Bible, but then also that's when all the distractions came. I believe because of my pain, because of the void in my life, losing my mother and no relationship with my biological father, made me a target. The devil used the need to be loved as a weapon against me. I began to look for love in all the wrong places. Numeral Uno the clubs.

Love Nots

Mommy's Death

4.

Self-Sabotage

I enjoyed the atmosphere because I knew how to dance. I had been dancing since the age of two and would close every party that my family had in the good old days. I refer to them as the good old days because although we were poor and there were episodes when the lights were cut off or the gas, our lives were happy. However, money was always present on a birthday or a holiday. My Mother, Grandma and Aunts would go broke to make sure that all the children had a Christmas tree and gifts under that tree.

There was always a feast for Thanksgiving and most importantly they celebrated birthdays. Everybody had a birthday party especially the adults. So at the birthday parties, I was always summoned to the living room to dance. I would entertain them and receive all the attention and praise that went mostly to my ego. This intoxication of getting attention followed me into my adulthood. So when Mom died, I assumed losing her would make James come back to me. I was sadly mistaken. After the funeral, I told my Dad that he was all that I had and that I needed him more than ever. He promised that he would be there for me. Not long after this conversation, he was once again in jail and I spiraled into a deep depression. I pretty much stayed in the house, only going to work. I remember about 6 months later, my cousins convinced me to get out the house and go downtown to this club.

Reluctantly, I decided to go. As we're driving down Joy road. I see this man hugging this woman walking down the street. It was Charles!!! I demanded that my cousin Joyce pull the car over. I jumped out the car, tears streaming down my face screaming at the top of my lungs. "He Killed My Mother!!!" Crying and hysterical, I was trying to fight him. "He Killed My Mama!!!" "He has AIDS" My cousins jumped out trying to get me back in the car. The woman looked confused. She asked him if he knew me. He denied knowing me.

I sobbed and cried hysterically. My cousins finally were able to get me in the car. "Turn the car around!" "Turn the car around." I repeated. "I don't want to go anymore." "Take Me home" "Take me home." I screamed. My cousins took me home. I told my Grandma. She didn't want to hear it. She was grieving herself and trying to still work and raise the children. I was exhausted, mentally and emotionally. I felt so alone. So eventually I turned to the night life and started to go out to the clubs. This went on for about a year. I found the club life fun and very exciting. It was a way of escape for me.

James was an outlet for me too. Although, he and I were split up, we saw each other periodically. This wasn't a sexual relationship, but it was almost, out of habit. Every Friday he would call me up and ask me out to a movie or out to eat. I was confused by his behavior. I misinterpreted his behavior, with him wanting me back. I was wrong. Every time I would bring the subject up or even hint at reconciling he would shut me down and reject me. That was so heartbreaking. It was if he was breaking my heart over and over again. But I was allowing it. James expressed repeatedly that he just wanted to be friends. In the process of this I was in school, barely. My grades suffered tremendously, I was there, but my mind was not. Finally, Dr. Reid suggested that I see a counselor at the University. This was after I explained to her the details behind my mother's death.

I made an appointment and went to see this counselor, which didn't help me at all. I cried during the entire session and none of my issues were resolved. Finally, under the recommendation of the University, I took a leave of absence from school. Before the leave, my friend Rhonda and I were bonding and hanging out more. We were always cool, but being at Wayne State together had gotten us closer. I would hang out at her house and found her brother to be really cute. He started making jokes about me growing up and not being a kid anymore. She seemed to be okay with it and encouraged him to call me. He was reluctant at first but decided to call. We had a really nice chat and he was impressed with my ability to have a mature conversation. I've known him since I was about 15 years old. I always admired him and thought he was cute. For some reason, I'm attracted to light or fair skinned men. He was a nice guy who wanted to be an actor and filmmaker. He was very talented, handsome, artistic and smart. I love the intelligent guys and I was drawn to his creativity. I started dating David in the Winter of 1990. We started talking on the phone more often. I knew that David and I were beginning to get serious, but I still had unresolved feelings for James.

I went to James one last time to be sure that there was nothing left. I apologized for the verbal abuse and everything I had done disrespectful in the relationship. I asked him if we could start over he replied no! That it was over. I said, "Ok" and got out of his car. A few days later David calls and wanted to take me out. Feeling rejected and alone, I agreed to go. We were intimate for the first time and nothing would be the same. He was absolutely crazy about me. Some people believe that he was a rebound and they're probably right. At that time, he was there for me because in my mind I had no one. My first love had abandoned me and David was there.

Shortly afterwards James called, I guess he was feeling guilty about the way things ended and wanted to check on me. He begins to question me and I told him that I had met someone and admitted that we had been intimate. He was so upset he was crying and hung up on me. I went to his house to try and talk to him, but that relationship was over. I had once again hurt him. All we did was hurt each other. For the life of me I couldn't understand why he was so hurt when he was so adamant about us not being together. I had made several attempts to reconcile our romance to no avail. So, I moved on with David and he was absolutely wonderful to me. I had never experienced a love like that. He was so attentive and protective of me. He really took care of me emotionally. We were inseparable. I could really talk to him. He was my best friend and lover. I was still dealing with the spirit of rejection with James and I was still having issues with my father.

David would comfort me, talk to me for hours, reassure me, build me up and just love me. I had never experienced loyalty like that before. He was such a wonderful friend and person. As time went on, my friendship with Rhonda became distant. I think a part of her resented me for coming into her brother's life. I don't think she expected for us to fall in love the way we did.

As crazy as it sounds, I tried several more times to reconnect with James, as a friend, but he was done with our relationship altogether. I finally gave up and decided to give David 100%. I'm so glad that I did. I had known him for years as my friend Rhonda's older brother. She really looked up to him and admired him, because he was the father figure in their family. He took care of everyone and he also took care of me. Although David and I were together, there were times I still felt like something was missing. I knew the death of my mother was still impacting my life, and that very well could have something to do with why I felt something was missing.

I began to hang out a lot with my friends and family. Going to the clubs and dancing, seem to relieve me, when I would get depressed about Mama. David would go out too sometimes. He loved to hang out at the techno clubs. I went with him a couple of times. The music was loud and you seem to get lost in it. I didn't particularly care for those clubs. They actually seemed weird. I remember one night we hung out at this club in downtown Detroit. Everyone was dancing, the music was loud and everyone seemed to be in a trance. There were images of things on the projector. One slide would be a picture of a rose or a water fall, and then the next slide would be an image of a demon with horns or something demonic. I thought I was imagining the images, but I was not. So, I stopped dancing and stared at the screen.

Sure, enough there were the subliminal images again. Let's just say, that was the last time I visited that club. I expressed my concerns to David and he eventually stopped hanging out there as well. After dating for a while, David proposed to me. I'll never forget it. It was my birthday and he came to my house and surprised me with a beautiful birthday cake. It read, Happy Birthday Ramona. I was absolutely elated. My Grandmother was there, so was my brother and cousins. We sang happy birthday and cut the cake. I was so ecstatic that he had done that for me. I felt *so* special. He had the entire night planned.

We went to a restaurant inside the Fisher building called Pegasus. It was really nice and upscale. As we sat there conversing and gazing into each other's eyes, I asked myself, "What had I done to deserve this wonderful guy?" He was so nice and sweet and he treated me with so much respect. After we placed our order, he told me that he had to go to the car. So I sat and waited. About 5 minutes later, he returned with this huge box, gift wrapped with this beautiful white bow. I was gleaming and smiling from ear to ear. "What have you done?" I asked. "I can't believe you did all this for me." He said. "Poo Bear, it's your birthday and you deserve this." I opened the box and there was a beautiful 2-piece gaucho set with necklace and bracelet to match.

I began to thank him for the cake, the gifts and dinner. He politely said. "Look deeper in the box" Huh? So I pulled back the tissue paper and there laid a smaller box under the clothes. I opened the box and there was a beautiful diamond ring. He told me that he loved me and that one day I would be his wife. I immediately put on the ring. I was engaged... I think... WE really didn't clarify when we would get married, just that we would. So as time moved on, my family knew, his family knew, but absolutely nothing was planned for this marriage.

As time passed, we became closer and closer and began to play house. That was a big mistake. David eventually moved out his mom's house and had his own apartment. He was working profusely on his acting career and even landed a television role on America's Most Wanted. Man, we thought he was a celebrity after that gig. I was in awe of him because he was such a go getter. He was also very romantic and attentive to me. My dad asked to meet him. I was surprised, but I made the arrangement.

He and David went out for drinks. My Dad approved of him and told him to take good care of me. I found out later from David, before they departed, my dad asked him to borrow 20.00 dollars. I was appalled. As time went on, he and I became more intimate. David was experienced and 5 years older than me. He knew a lot about sex and he was also a hopeless romantic himself. He believed in the flowers, candy and he absolutely loved to watch movies. It was during this time I began to feel a pull to God, so I joined Chapel Hill Church. I didn't really know anything about the church. I just remember seeing it whenever I would ride the Joy road bus.

I didn't understand the bible at all either. Nonetheless, I would try to read it. I just couldn't comprehend the thee, thy and thous. So, I put it down. I joined and got baptized, but I didn't even know what that really meant. I just knew that I went down in the water with a long white gown on and came up. No one in my family was in church, so I thought it would be nice to invite everyone to my baptismal. I also invited David and he came to see me get baptized. I invited my family, but they went to the Miller picnic instead.

This was a family tradition in Black Bottom. That was a part of my Grandmother's heritage and a family tradition, so we went every year. I was baptized on a Sunday at evening service. I went in the water and I came out the water. After the baptism, I really didn't go back. I didn't feel a real connection there. As the months passed, David and I became settled. We stopped hanging out and spent a lot of time relaxing and watching movies. Before long, I was pregnant. I was scared, humiliated and very disappointed in myself. I had been on the pill since I was 16 years old and I had become extremely careless with taking them properly. I remember the night that I told him.

I was working at the Mobil gas station on Dexter. That gas station hired everybody. All my friends were working there Kia, Shellie and Rena. I dreaded letting him know, but I knew that I had too. I wasn't trying to live the life that my mom lived, but here I was. I had dropped out of college, and my life was in limbo. When I told David, he immediately informed me that he wasn't ready to be a father. I was devastated. I thought because we were engaged that he would be happy, but that was not the case. I told David on a Thursday and by Monday, he'd taken the money out of his account and we were at the clinic.

I was numb. He took off that day. We filled out the paper work and then he left. He later returned and picked me up. This clinic was in the Penobscot Building. It's funny, I would have never thought that a place like that would be located in such a prominent and historical building downtown. A friend of mine told me about this place. It was cold, damp and impersonal. No conversations and all the women looked like zombies; we were all in another world. Our minds filled with doubt and shame. I felt horrible.

I kept the pregnancy a secret from my immediate family. No one knew accept a few close cousins. I was humiliated and very sad. After terminating my pregnancy, I never looked at David quite the same. Our relationship changed immediately! I didn't understand, if he says he loves me and I am wearing his ring, why didn't he want me and our child? That feeling of rejection resurfaced and it brought back all those feelings about my mother and Father. I recuperated at my Aunt's house. My Aunt and cousins took care of me and before long I was ok physically, although severely altered spiritually, mentally and emotionally. I became detached that day. I was never the same. I wanted my child, but I was a 21-year-old college dropout working at a gas station. There was a house full of children because my Grandma still had not only Aunt Bunnies' children, but now my two brothers. I couldn't burden her with a baby.

I buried my sorrow and depression in drinking and partying. I found myself starting to hang out more and more again. I was hitting the clubs with my cousins quite frequently. I was trying to forget all my pain and drown it out with the night life. I was still dealing with my mother's death and now feeling the guilt and shame of terminating a pregnancy. I began to distance myself from David. It was the beginning of the end. The clubs were fun!!! Boy did I enjoy myself; I didn't have to think about the struggles and sadness of my life or family.

It was a way to escape, so I went to what has always been familiar to me. My mind wasn't on home, returning to school or pretty much anything. I was still curious about God though, but it wasn't enough for me to stop hanging out. As a matter of fact, I started hanging out more and more with my cousins. I didn't want to be home because it was too much of a reminder of the loss and emptiness in the house. This put a horrible strain on David's and I relationship. The evitable happened. I cheated on him.

I met Robert at Soul Night. Soul night was held once a month at the State Theater in Detroit. It was the party of the month and everybody attended. We would spend a month coordinating our outfits for that one night. So anyway, it was Soul night and my cousin Maya and I were coming up the stairs and there he was. Tall, pretty caramel skin, wearing a hat with the continent of Africa on it, with a medallion to match. Our eyes met and he said Hi. I said, "I love a man that's into his culture." He smiled and my heart skipped a beat. He had the most profound dimples. He asked me my name and if I was alone. I introduced myself and also my cousin.

He follows us up the stairs. He then introduces his best friend Jeff to Maya and it was love at first sight for them. Robert and I instantly clicked. He was fun and he made me laugh. He told me that he wanted to get married one day and looked forward to having his own family. I liked that, especially after what just transpired with David. We talked on the phone constantly and I was instantly drawn to him. He was charismatic and very intelligent. I really enjoyed our conversations because he stimulated me mentally and intellectually. He fascinated me because he was articulate and romantic. He also loved to party.

My cousins thought that he was fine and cool. He *was* good looking. Robert had a presence. When he walked in a room, you knew he was there. He owned it and was extremely confident. Some may mistake this confidence for arrogance or cockiness. Jeff really liked Maya, so when they started dating, that increased our connection because they were always around. Hanging out with us, meeting us at the club and then we started planning get togethers at my cousins' house. He never questioned whether I was in a relationship and to be truthful I never told him.

I liked him. Robert was a Gemini like me, so he loved to communicate and we would talk for hours. He attended Wayne State and I lied and told him I was there too, which I wasn't. I had left during this time. David knew something wasn't right. I would stand him up and became unavailable for holidays and other important dates. I never confessed to David because I didn't want to hurt him. He was really a good guy, but I had become really detached from him. To be honest, I believed that David would eventually leave me. So I built a wall to protect myself. Slowly my heart was becoming more callous. I knew eventually my double life would catch up with me.

One night, David came to Soul Night. I looked up and I was staring him in the face. Hi baby, so this is Soul Night! I figured my lady is always down here maybe I need to check it out. I was speechless. I was in shock. I came up with an excuse to leave for a moment. I ran up to my cousin Joyce and said very slowly, "David is here". She quickly went into control mode. Okay, you need to get sick now! "Who do you want me to send to the van?" I told her to send Robert. At that moment David and I were over. I think that night he knew as well. He never uttered a word about it.

I knew Robert was not good for me. We were beginning to argue, the first one started that night. He found it very suspicious that I was fine one minute ago and all of a sudden now I'm sick. He questioned me in the van, which turned into an argument because I believe he knew that I was involved with someone. We argued about various things, especially his health. He was diabetic and I was really concerned about his health. He would drink 2-liter Mountain Dews all the time, as well as beer. I constantly stressed my views on the matter. After a few months of dating he decides to join a fraternity. That's when everything changed. He explained to me the severity of the matter and that he would need me to be very patient. He assured me that he would make it up to me in the end. Robert and I were not able to see one another as much.

While pledging, he would attempt to make time to see me, but he was always tired. More and More his life began to change, he'd even became more distant with Jeff. The night he crossed he was ecstatic. I was extremely happy for him and thought that we could finally get back on track. He called and asked to see me. I was at my Aunt's and he came by. We slow danced in the basement to Baby Come Close by Smokey Robinson. That was our song along with Just Me and You by Tone Tone Tone. The connection was still there and he promised to spend more time with me now that he had crossed. It never happened. His life became a whirlwind with parties and step shows and before long, he was a magnet for women. Let me clarify, he was always a magnet, but it intensified when he became an Alpha.

My good friend Joseph was already an Alpha and once he found out that I was seeing Robert, he informed me that Robert was dating an AKA. I confronted him about the situation and he twisted everything and was upset with his frat brother. Many of them believed that Joseph betrayed the brotherhood. So he was dating me and her and because I was no longer in his circle, it was hard for me to catch him in his lies. Once this triangle surfaced, it was upsetting. I started to get prank calls and I wasn't sure if it was from her or maybe he was putting individuals up to calling. So I broke it off with him.

It wasn't easy leaving him alone because he was such a player that he would call all night long leaving messages saying, "I love you and I miss you", I'm sorry. "Please call me." "Ramona, Ramona, Ramona." He loved to call my name. I actually never liked my name until I met Robert. I thought it sounded old. I guess I had no right to be hurt or upset. I needed to get over it and move on. I was sabotaging my relationship with David for a guy that wasn't even worth it. What sense did that make?

I was making terrible decisions, there was no stability in my life. One night there was an Alpha party at Wayne State and I convinced my friend Theresa to go with me. I wore a black and gold jean outfit. It was sharrrp!! Theresa fixed my hair in a French roll with the spiral curls hanging on the side. My shoes were black and gold heels. I was too cute. I came purposely to start trouble. I was tired of the calls and the accusations, so I wanted to witness Robert's new life up close and personal.

When we walked in I saw the young lady that he was dating. I knew it was her because of the name on her jacket. Someone recognizes me and spoke and from her reaction she realized who I was. I was a live wire and I knew exactly what I was doing. I was curious about her and also wanted to see if he was lying to me with his long-winded messages. So, yes this was a test to see if it was all bullshit. I saw my friend Joseph and he hugged me. He was such a nice guy and very handsome. I just wasn't attracted to him in that way. He was my friend, my confidant and I trusted his judgment. We danced and Robert watched us on the floor. Eventually he came over and spoke to me. I was cordial, smiled and engaged in his small talk. He complimented me on my outfit and told me that I looked really nice. His girl was in a huddle with her sisters and didn't like our interaction with each other. I suggested that he get back to his girlfriend. I could see that my presence had everyone uncomfortable.

The two of them start to dance. The song changes and all of a sudden, "Just me and you" comes on. Now, that song had been out for a while, so I'm not sure if he requested it, but I certainly didn't. I guess it was the devil being busy or maybe a coincidence, but all I see is Robert walking across the floor to me. He grabs me and says. "You know I have to dance with you right. This is our song." So we dance and his girl is having a breakdown in the corner. Then she comes over to us and demands that he gets off the floor. "Get off the floor!" Get off the floor!"

He tells her he's dancing and that she needs to go and sit down. I say to him, you need to go and be with your girl. That's your girl, right? Before he can answer, his frat brothers are rushing over to him and badgering him about his behavior. Remember it's not only a brotherhood, it's a family and their sister was hurt. I found out what I needed to know and I left. Was I proud of myself? No, I wasn't. My ego was bruised and I went there to prove a point. In the end, we were both being played and for the most part, I was in a relationship. I was just as bad as Robert, but there was no moment to pause and turn things around. I was too far gone… I didn't want to talk to David. I secretly resented him.

I believe subconsciously, I wanted to punish him for his rejection of me and my pregnancy. All this was from a place of hurt. Things escalated. I was selfish. I should have just released him. That was the noble thing to do. I knew deep down that he was a good guy and I was keeping him around hoping that we could get our love back. But the relationship was damaged, because I was damaged. I wasn't going to be vulnerable with him or confess to him my feelings of rejection. No! Not this time. I wasn't ready to face the truth.

Instead of facing my personal demons and my problems at home, I ran from them. I went out seeking the attention from men. I seem to attract the low lives, the cheaters, and the men that lived in their mother's basements. I guess it's true, you attract what you are. Because at that time, I had no self-esteem and I needed constant validation. It was clear. I wasn't moving forward in my life. I had dropped out of Wayne State and I wasn't counseled to withdraw my classes. As a result, I owed the school over 2,000 dollars and I went into a deeper depression. So yes, you do attract what you are because in my mind, I was a failure. So this is the state of mind I was in when I went to church on August 23rd 1993.

Love Nots

Self-Sabotage

5.

Life of Christ

My first experience with the presence and anointing of God was awesome. Breathtaking, I might add. I had never felt anything like that in my life. I wanted more and more. I was 23 years old and in a tumultuous relationship. This guy Gino seemed to be the devil himself. But I'm sure you are picturing a very unattractive guy with a bad attitude. On the contrary he was handsome, well dressed, poised, but was the biggest con artist you would ever meet. He was extremely charismatic which made him a magnet for women. I absolutely loved him. After experiencing so much rejection, I actually believed he was a prize based on what, his looks? Would this guy love me, really love me? This poor, nappy head girl from the ghetto. The devil is cunning. He uses our insecurities to trap us. Anyway, this relationship was so bad, that by the time I had my first meeting with God, I was walking around looking like a crackhead due to all the arguing, pain, being cheated on and cussed out. Need I say more. I was fed up and stressed out from this guy. He had me on an emotional roller-coaster and it was time to get off. My childhood friend Shellie invited me to her church that she'd recently joined, Great Faith Ministries International. I remember it like it was yesterday, it was on a Friday night in a "Miracles do happen" service. I was reluctant to go because well, you know the excuse. I don't have anything to wear. I was what you call, back in the day a "hoochie mama," a party girl. Any party that was going on in the city, you bet I was there and with a new outfit on.

I was determined to go to this church service. I really enjoyed the preaching. I believe Bishop Jackson, back then was Pastor Jackson, is truly a man of God. I believe God sent him to Detroit for people like me. For individuals who come from dysfunctional families and broken homes, who need to experience the manifestation of the true living God. It is not a coincidence that Great Faith Ministries International is located in the area that it's in. God knew that his people needed deliverance and they needed to experience miracles and know that he is real.

In this area, there are many who are hopeless and filled with despair. Every corner there is a liquor store and on every block, there is a crack house. People were giving up, and people were numb, because of their circumstances. I was one of those people. During that time in the early 1990's. I had let's review: Dropped out of college at Wayne State University, worked a dead-end job at Mobil gas station and had moved at least 3 times in 3 years.

When I went to church, I had not been delivered or set free from the pain of losing my mother. I still had many issues at that time and I was very angry and lonely. Four years had passed and I was *still* hurting. God knew that I needed deliverance, but I didn't. I had no clue what deliverance meant. That was language that was foreign to me because no one in my immediate family attended church. I went to church and wore a white move something dress. Oh my, I'm laughing just thinking about how ridiculous I felt in that dress. That was all I had to wear, but I was determined to go anyway. God says to come as you are, it doesn't matter what apparel you have on.

I was fed up and tired of all the heartache and I was expecting to come out of that service, feeling better. The service was awesome and I couldn't stop crying. I didn't understand why I was crying so much. The choir was awesome, and the praise and worship team was unbelievable. These people were clapping their hands and stomping their feet. They were dancing, I could not believe my eyes. People were running around the church and happy. I have never been to a church and witnessed individuals praising God in this manner. Some were crying, but it wasn't from sadness. Many were reverencing God and lifting their hands in acknowledgement of God. I was confused as to what was happening, but I knew

I wanted something they had. I was certainly at peace.

I was truly overwhelmed and for the moment, happy and not focusing on my problems. It was the end of service and I will never forget it. Bishop had an altar call and I remember wanting to get up. My legs felt like lead. I couldn't move. I felt the weight of the world on me. I remember thinking, if I get up, people are going to judge me and look at my dress and say, "Look at that girl, where does she think she is at, the club?" So I stayed in my seat. I know it was a trick of the enemy. But the saints of God, must be careful, because there are people who need to be saved and set free and the saints sometimes look at them like they are unworthy of being saved. It is always wise to remember that, "You have to catch the fish before you can scale the fish." But because of self-righteous people, souls are lost, because of how we treat people based on what they look like or how they are dressed.

We are created in His image and we are joint heirs with Jesus Christ. We *should* look and dress appropriately, but there are those who don't have the resources, finances or even know what appropriate is and are in need of guidance. Our focus should be winning souls, not what they are wearing, at least not initially. I believe this should be addressed in churches, especially on the airwaves and on television to come as you are. Just come! As they are being discipled in the things of God, in most cases you don't have to tell anyone that they need to dress modestly or appropriately because the Holy Spirit will bring conviction to them.

Pastor Jackson asked, if there was anyone who wanted the Holy Ghost. I really didn't know what that entailed, but before I knew it, I was running down to the altar. It was a plea and a cry for help. Although, I was a bit unsure what the Holy Ghost was, I *was* familiar with the terminology and it was always expressed in a manner to be something good. As I walked across the altar, I could hear the people clapping and shouting Hallelujah, so I knew I had made a positive decision. As I was led to the back of the church, Pastor stopped me and he proceeded to give me a "Word of knowledge".

He begins to tell me things about my life. He mentioned my relationship that I was in and the fact that men had hurt me. He begins to tell me about the dysfunction and chaos that was occurring in my home. As he spoke to me I remember wondering, "How does this man know these things about me?" I have never spoken to him before. I don't know him and he doesn't know me. He explained that God through the Holy Spirit revealed these things to him. He said. "Daughter I don't know who you are or who brought you here. But God told me to tell you He loves you." As I heard these words, tears began to run down my face. "God loves me?" I thought. He loves me? After all the things I've done? All the partying and being involved in bad relationships and indulging in sexual sin? "God loves *me*?"

It was if Pastor Jackson could read my thoughts or maybe he just read the expression on my face.

Because he repeated, "Yes, God Loves you. He then told me that God wanted to give me peace. He explained that when he laid his hands on me, that God was going to touch me from the top of my head to the soles of my feet. He explained that it was not him that he was just a vessel that God was going to use to make the contact. He gave all the Glory to God. He also told me that the spirit of depression that was on me was going to be broken and that I will never be the same. He then laid hands on my forehead and all I remember is falling out. I was not forced down or pushed down. He laid his hands on my forehead and I hit the floor. I was informed later that the power was so strong that Shellie fell out as well, and she was in the back of the church.

I remember feeling a peace that I had never felt my whole life. It was if I had an out of body experience. There was a place in me that was touched that had never been touched before. I know now that it was my spirit that was touched, made alive to God and His love poured into my heart. His love began to affect me in ways I could never imagine. It was if God had literally wrapped His arms around me. I felt heat and I remember feeling so happy and at peace. I laid there for a long time crying and just embellishing in the presence of God that I had never experienced before. This was new, but I knew it was real.

I must admit, before this experience, I had watched television ministries and I was guilty of being one of those skeptics that said, "That's fake." "They pushed those people down." Don't get me wrong, there are people out there that push people down but its only because they want us to think that it's the power of God. In my case, it *was* the power of God! It's very real. God is real and it felt *so good,* to be in the presence of my Heavenly Father to feel His love, to cry out to Him about all of my sorrow. I had yearned for the love of a father for so long and I didn't know how the lack of a father's love could screw me up so badly. I was His daughter and it had been revealed to me that He loved me. That I was loved and that I was worthy.

I could hear the people in the congregation, but they sounded far away. The noise was faint. It was as if I was somewhere else. Because I was. God is Spirit and so are we. Spirit, soul and body. And at that moment my spirit connected to God, like an umbilical cord attached to its mother, a tether of sorts, connecting me to the healing and deliverance, I so desperately needed. That night I was baptized and received the Holy Ghost. The head mother and intercessor of the church had to work vigorously for me to receive. She had to tarry with me. I remember she kept saying "LOOSE HER!" She repeated that over and over again. It was difficult for me to receive the evidence of speaking in other tongues. I know now that Satan didn't want to let me go! I was the first in my immediate family to receive The Gift. The Devil knew generational curses would be broken and that I would intercede for my family. Finally, after tarrying for about 20 minutes mother shouted, "Take Her to The Water!"

I informed her that I had already been baptized. She said. "You need another dip!" So I was baptized again and received the Holy Ghost with the evidence of speaking in other tongues that night. My life would never be the same. The scriptures state in John 3:16, *For God so loved the world that he gave his only begotten son, that whosoever believe in him shall not perish, but have everlasting life.* I was saved! I'm not saying that everything became peaches and cream after that. On the contrary, that's when the real battle began. That's when Satan decided that he really wanted to try and destroy me. I made a decision that night to serve God. I met my Heavenly Father for the first time. It was beautiful and we talked all night. I prayed and meditated and cried some more, but it was okay because I had a lot to say and cry about.

Tears can act as a cleansing and I needed to disinfect my spirit. So much rejection, and hurt had been deposited in my spirit. So much self-doubt and words spoken out against me to curse my spirit had been deposited in me. So it was time to detox. It was time to get rid of all the waste. God wanted to heal and deliver me from all of it. The Lord wanted to heal the pain from my father rejecting me as a child and my mother resenting me for it. The pain of losing my mother and the mental anguish I suffered because of her death. Jesus wanted to heal me in those secret places of shame and condemnation of allowing my body, my temple, to be used for sexual gratification in ungodly relationships. Looking for love in all the wrong places and not having the revelation of God's love. Therefore, displaying a false representation of love for myself, attracting the most selfish-self-centered egotistical, "you need to be glad I'm even with you," type of men." I had a good cleansing, but I was still a work in progress.

Love Nots

6.

You've Been Warned

Gino was fine, he was brown skinned slim and could dance. This is the relationship that I was in when I received Christ in 1993. Our courtship was like a whirlwind. Let me give you the timespan. We actually met in 1991, but I didn't really know him. We were in the same club circles, but were not friends. He had his friends and I had mine and family that I hung out with. Our scene was Maxi's, we were like local celebrities there. When we walked into Maxi's, everyone knew us. We had our own table and it was always empty, because they knew not to sit there. We walk in at least 9 or 10 deep every Monday night. My cousins Joyce, Celeste, Maya and the crew. We were hanging like wet clothes. Those days were crazy and fun. At least I thought so. I realize now, all I was doing was running from my pain and not facing my problems. Clubbing was a way of escape for me. The devil is a liar. When you really think about it, most people that are always in the clubs are running from something. Think about it, you're there week after week for what? Seeing the same people, the same faces, for what? Because most likely you're hiding from something. You don't want to face reality and the club is a fantasy world that you can create for yourself. At least it was for me. You're important, you're like a local celebrity. Especially if you can dance like me.

I thought I was all that and a bag of chips, with dip and a coke on the side to wash it all down. At least when I was buzzing, because when I wasn't…I was deeply insecure. The alcohol was liquid courage. It was the 90's when John Singleton's, Boys in the Hood hit the screen. Everybody was in love with Cuba Gooding Jr. and Morris "chocolate fine" Chestnut. Our drink of choice was St. Ides and Blue Motherf@#&ers. I can't even write that word now. Anyway, back to Boys in The Hood. I loved that movie because it gave the raw unadulterated truth about what goes on in the hood. I was a girl from the hood…. Dexter, Linwood, Joy Road, loyal friendships, partying, dysfunctional families and yes even tragedy. Everyone had hopes and dreams of someday leaving the hood. The truth is, whether you are fortunate to leave the hood or not. The hood is always in you. It's a part of you! It can define you at times. That's why that movie impacted everyone, because it spoke volumes.

Anyway, my days of hanging out were full and plenty. Maxi's on Mondays. Soul Night once a month on Tuesdays. Wednesdays was Chucks Millionaires Club on Plymouth and Babes on Saturday. I was very absorbed with myself and had become very selfish. Some would even say I was a b@#$h! I loved the attention that I received at the clubs. More and more I didn't see David. He was hurt and didn't understand my attitude. I was changing, my heart was hardening toward him and I was heavily influenced by my new lifestyle. I was running! Running from myself, running from God, and running from my family. Just running and lost. I had a false sense of confidence. In order for it to thrive, it had to remain in that atmosphere.

January winter of 1993 Gino and I became reacquainted. I was out one night at Club International. The music was bumping, but the club was empty. It was a snowstorm that night and no one was there. I saw Gino wearing a long black leather coat on the floor dancing. We made eye contact. We knew one another from hanging in the same clubs. He walked over and asked me to dance. Gino was also a good dancer and we danced a couple of songs straight that night. We worked that dance floor. A slow song came on, No Rhyme No Reason and we slow danced. We laughed, we talked and had fun that night. It was the most we had ever talked.

After the club closed and I was leaving, he stopped me and handed me his business card. He told me that he tinted windows and asked if he could call me sometimes. I gave him my number. He called that night to make sure that I arrived home safely. We ended up talking on the phone for about an hour. Every day we talked more and more. Before I knew it, we were seeing each other. David and I were still together, we had not officially broken up. But were no longer intimate or hanging out. He pleaded with me to explain what changed. Finally, I told him that I needed some space and needed to work some things out. I could not continue to hurt him so we finally split up. I didn't feel any pain or guilt. I have no idea why? I never thought of myself as so heartless. I felt betrayed by him still. He decided to give me the space. That left time for Gino and me to get to know one another better. We hung out for two weeks straight. From Belle Isle hanging on the strip, to the movies, the drive in, and Greek town. We went everywhere. Gino drove a white Mustang that he absolutely worshipped. He loved that car. You could hear him coming a mile away. He had amps in the car and the music, would be bumping. Gino and I both fell really hard for one another.

He had a little boy that was a toddler and I absolutely adored him. Gino assured me that he was over his child's mother. He explained that they were no longer together because she cheated on him and hurt him very badly. I wanted to ease that hurt. I connected with him because I had been hurt as well. First, by James and then by David. One evening David popped over my house. I looked up and he was standing in my bedroom door. One of my little cousins had let him in. I was speechless. He came into my room and immediately saw a picture of Gino on my wall. He was crushed. "So who is this guy?" I didn't know how to respond. He asked me again "So who is this guy?" I told him that Gino was my friend. It's only been two weeks and a picture of your friend is on your wall. He got up and left. All I remember is seeing him walking down the street with his head down. I felt horrible. He didn't deserve to be hurt in that way. Hurt people hurt people. It's a vicious cycle and I was hurting. Though he had shown up without calling first. I guess that's what can happen.

My family had moved yet again and I hated where we lived. During this time, I was living in a little house that leaned to the side. No, I am not exaggerating. The house literally leaned to the side, we could have called it "The leaning house of Pisa", to the right, to be exact. My bedroom door had a star on it. I'm not sure if it was a pentagon devil star or not. I was scared though, so I scrubbed the pentagram off my door with bleach. I got it off too. I shouted! "OH MY GOD, DEVIL WORSHIPPERS LIVED IN THIS HOUSE". Grandma just started cussing and said, "Scrub the damn star off!" So that's what I did.

There were guys that sold drugs that lived across the street from us. I didn't have anything to do with anyone. They all thought I was stuck up. I didn't care. My Grandmother treated them nice because my brother and cousins were young and she didn't want them to try to recruit them. She still was working and it was still a struggle. I had left the gas station on Dexter and had transferred to the one on Grand River. I was working the afternoon shift and trying to help out as much as I could.

Gino lived on the eastside of Detroit and traveled every night from the east side to the west side to pick me up from work. We were inseparable. As time passed. Gino began to show signs of being emotionally unstable. He had a really bad temper at times. I remember one day his car broke down and we were stranded far east. Gino started punching his car with his fists which made his knuckles bleed. His pager went off constantly and it really irritated me. I knew women were attracted to him. Because he was very charming and very good looking. He had the most beautiful light brown eyes. When Gino was in his good mood, he made me feel as if I was the only woman on earth. He would come to the house bumping Mary J Blige's, I'm The Only Woman and jump out the car and literally pick me up, spin me around and say, "Baby Girl." That was his nickname for me. I loved him so much. I loved the potential that I saw in him. He was fun fun fun. We always laughed and we'd just ride and cruise the streets of Detroit. With the music blasting, the windows down in the summertime, we just cruised.

Sometimes we would pick his mom up from work and hang out with his friends. I didn't care for any of his friends though. They were younger and seemed very immature. I didn't understand why he felt the need to hang out with this young bunch. He also had his club friends, but as we got closer he saw them less and less. I wasn't worried though because we were together all the time. I met his mother, who really didn't care for mc. Gino was a mama's boy. His mother paged him all day long. He had a sister, but she was really quiet most of the time. His mother went to church and was a singer. They were from Louisiana and Gino told me that his father was Creole and the family spoke French. Gino also told me that his mom expressed to him there were ways to get control of people with voodoo. I didn't believe any of it though. My Grandmother was another story.

Because of my Grandmother's history with her step mother, she was leery of Gino's family. My Grandmother's step mother practiced witchcraft, so she was very suspicious of them. My Grandma would tell us stories about her evil Stepmother. Grandma lost her mom, my Great Grandmother Laura Lou, at the age of 11. After her death, this woman came to the house, married her father and treated her and her siblings horribly. The lady even fed them separate food and stored strange things in jars in the attic. That's one of the reasons Grandma married so young, to get away from her Stepmother.

Gino's Mom and my Grandmother did not get along at all. She didn't approve and wanted me to run away from him and his family as fast as I could. We had countless arguments about him. She didn't like him and didn't want me to date him. She actually loved David though. Everyone did. He was just a respectful nice and cool person, in everyone's eyes. But back to Gino. As the relationship progressed, I started to notice some things about him. There were long periods of time where he would just disappear. Time unaccounted for. I would page him and it would take hours for him to respond. Then we began to argue a lot. Our relationship became like a roller coaster. It was very passionate; our arguments and fights would be full of rage. Within an hour of all that arguing, we would make love. It was crazy. I was definitely a fool in love.

This relationship was different from my previous relationships. Gino was more like me. He argued, he was hyper, he could dance, and he joked and loved the club. We had a lot more in common and he didn't judge me. I didn't have to be perfect with him and neither did I have to tame my personality. I was a fireball and he *loved* it. I could just be me, with all my faults, craziness and feistiness. He loved *me*. I did find out that Gino lied to me about how many children he had. There was a picture of a big eyed little boy in his bedroom that I found. He acknowledged it was a child that a female accused him of being the father, but his mom said the child wasn't his. I was baffled. He admitted that he was intimate with her, but claimed the child wasn't his. I asked. "How would his mother know that?" Did she lay down and have sex with the female or did Gino? That is absurd. We argued about it and he took me home. The toddler appeared to be about 2 years old the same age as his son.

I later found out that the child was also named Gino. He had two children who were both Gino junior, that were about 6 months apart. He wasn't in the little boy's life and it was disheartening. I believed him when he told me otherwise. I guess I didn't want to think that he could be so heartless and abandon his child. He absolutely cherished his first-born Gino Jr. and seemed to be a good father to him. So I believed the lie. As the relationship continued, his other side appeared more and more.

One day I got the call. My phone ranged and it was a young lady on the line. She told me that she and Gino had been seeing each other and that they had been intimate. I was devastated. She told me that she was 18 years old and lived down the street from him. Apparently, he fell asleep and she looked at his pager and saw my number and the multiple pages back and forth. I was a mess and distraught. How could he do this to me? Gino thrived on attention, he craved it. He loved when others bragged on his car, his clothes, or his dancing. I confronted him. It was dramatic. I cried, he cried. It was very emotional. I broke up with Gino that night. I told him that I could never take him back. He called, I would hang up. He paged, I wouldn't answer. It was painful, but it was over.

Summer 1993 I started working at Marianne's Downtown. It was a retail clothing store for women. I had finally left the gas station and started working there. I loved that job. I loved how busy it was and the hustle and bustle of the people. I met some wonderful young ladies who worked there too. Anyway, he would call my job and the ladies would protect me and tell him I was off or busy. I couldn't concentrate. I didn't know if I was coming or going. I had decided about a month prior to his cheating, to audition for the Detroit-Windsor Dance Academy, which was a company that was doing big things in Detroit. This was something that I was waiting on for a while. Especially, since I was no longer in school. I was in great anticipation for this chance.

It just happened to be the week that all this occurred. I went to the audition and was a mess. The dancing was not polished and sloppy. I even forgot choreography. I was awkwardly nervous and my countenance was sad. I was broken. I didn't get accepted. They told me to work on some things and come back. This was the first audition I failed at. I was disappointed. Gino, had flowers delivered to my job every day for a week. He was beginning to wear me down. Finally, after much persistence I decided to see him. We met at Nikki's Pizza in Greektown. Gino hadn't seen me in about 3 weeks.

I was so thin and so stressed. He cried when he saw me because I was so skinny. I had loss about 10 lbs. I weighed about 105 lbs during this time. I was nothing, but head and eyes. It hurt him to see me in that condition. I was so hurt that it took my appetite. I couldn't even eat the pizza that we ordered. Gino realized the severity of his betrayal because I absolutely loved to eat. We talked and cried together, but I didn't take him back. After about a month of trying to get me to go out with him. I gave in. He planned this romantic night for me. He took me to dinner at this Japanese restaurant off the river. We had to take off our shoes and sit on the floor. I had never been to a place like that before; He began to express his love for me and told me that he wanted to marry me. After some persuasion, I decided to give him another chance. He promised that he would never hurt me like that again. I believed him. It was beautiful and we were happy for a minute.

He gave me this beautiful diamond ring. I was told by his friends that he bust his butt to get me that ring. Shortly, we were back at it. The lying, the temper tantrums, this was the same old Gino. One day, we got into it really bad. And he demanded I get out of his car. I thought he was joking but he wasn't. So me being the feisty person I was, I did. I wasn't far from home, but it was the audacity of him to put me out. That was it for me, at least I thought. I walked home and cried the whole way there. Something had to change and the change was me. I couldn't believe it, after everything he promised. I was back to square one *again*. This incident led to the night I got saved!

After giving my life to Christ. Everything changed. I had a new outlook on life. My family thought I had lost my mind. I started talking to them about God all the time. I even told them they were going to hell if they didn't change their ways. They thought I was a fanatic. I guess I was. I really did seem crazy to them. I had not found balance with my new revelation. God is a God of love. He is not an accuser. The devil is the accuser. God draws with love. I was berating everyone. So it was hard for the Lord to use me. I did get a few of my friends to join the church though.

My childhood friend Kelly and her mother joined. My friend Carol also joined and so did her brother. Also, my best male friend Joseph joined and even became an usher. As well as my two cousins and brother, they were baptized there. I told everyone about the church, even my ex's. I told Robert and he laughed and James they both declined. I was spreading the Gospel of Jesus Christ. I absolutely loved Great Faith Ministries. Although, it was a huge church with many members, I loved the fact that the Pastors personally knew me.

When I wasn't there or missed service, Pastor Jackson was definitely aware. Sometimes he would say. "Ramona, you weren't in bible study Tuesday." That was important to me because it showed that he was concerned about his sheep. For the first time in a long time, I was a part of something positive and great. I had not felt like I belonged anywhere in years. It was a great feeling. I was so grateful to my friend Shellie for inviting me to church that evening. It changed my life. She played an integral role in my walk with God and I will never forget it. I had expressed to Gino that I could no longer live in sexual sin with him. I told him that it was over and that I was saved. He did not understand the change in me. I wanted to learn about God and was fed up with the direction of my life. It was still all new to me, but I was eager to learn. Guess what? Gino showed up at my church. He even joined and was baptized. It was prophesied that he had a call on his life to preach the Gospel and that God wanted to use him. He was coming to church faithfully and I was beginning to see a life with him. That was until Sweetest Day 1993.

Gino and I had made plans and I paged and called and paged and call. I couldn't reach him. The next day at church he showed up. I was livid. He claimed that he had been in jail all night. That he went to pick up a gift for me and was pulled over by the Dearborn police. There was a warrant for tickets and he was arrested. He said that he spent the night in jail. I was mad, but then I thought, well at least he came to church. After service we spoke outside, He asked me to walk to his car. Inside he had a beautiful box, gift wrapped in the back seat. I opened the box there was a beautiful silk scarf, skirt and blouse set and a pager with a hot pink case. All was forgiven and we were once again in love. When I found out I was pregnant, we both were so happy. He and I hadn't been sexually intimate since me joining the church. I wanted to see if he was just playing church.

We didn't know how to break the news to our pastors. We needed to know how to handle the situation. Gino trusted a brother at the church and confided in him for advice. This brother told him to ask for a meeting to discuss our situation. Gino wanted to talk to our Pastor himself. So that we could get married and explain that the baby was conceived before I came to the church. We were not ashamed, we were not hiding. We both honestly just needed a little guidance. We were really trying to do this the right way. We both were excited about the ministry and wanted to really change. The desire was there, we just didn't know how to do it. Gino never got that conversation. The brother from the church went back and told our leaders before we could. Gino was very upset and started to talk against the church. Because he believed that confidentiality and trust was broken. He vowed to never go back. It was Thanksgiving and Gino's family knew that I was expecting. His family wasn't pleased at all. I could feel the tension at the table. Gino's mother and sister constantly brought up his son's mother.

They talked about how they switched roles for Halloween one year. That she dressed as a man and he as a woman. I found it to be terribly disrespectful, but he didn't see it. They wanted to upset me and didn't like the fact that I was having his child. After dinner, he took me home. We argued because I expressed my hurt and concerns. Later that night. I started to spot. I called Gino and he took me to Receiving Hospital. I lost the baby. I was 12 weeks. The doctor performed a D and C and I was discharged. I was heartbroken. I believed that God had taken my child because of my previous sin. I believed that he hadn't forgiven me.

Sister Carolyn from the church contacted me and sent a card. She told me that she was praying for me and that I needed to come back to church. Also, Sister Deborah, who was an angel that God connected me to also, picked me up every Sunday for church, when I first got saved. She was always praying for me. No one else contacted me. I assumed they knew about my miscarriage. I went to church a few weeks later hurt, angry and upset that no one in leadership had contacted me. I didn't know anything about church protocol. I didn't know I was supposed to contact them. I assumed they knew. I approached my Pastor in the hall. He asked me how I was doing and where I had been. I told him that I wasn't good and that I had loss the baby. I was sad, angry and felt alone. He asked why didn't I let anyone know. I began to say to him that a few people knew and why should I have to call them. They were the church and should check on their members. After going back and forth for a minute. A small crowd came in the hall.

Pastor tells me that I shouldn't be with Gino! "He is NOT the man that God has for you." He said. I was furious. "You don't know him." "How can you judge him?" I replied. "Well, he's sleeping with you and you're not married. That's not a man of God." I was devastated! Tears went streaming down my face. Finally! He saw my tears and I could see the compassion in his eyes. "Where's your Mama?" he asked. "She's dead!!!" I screamed! Then Pastor asked, "Where's your father?" "I don't know," I replied! Sobbing… Pastor Jackson grabbed me and hugged me. He then took me to the Word. He opened up the Bible to James 5:14, 15. He explained to me that anytime I am weary, sick etc… I should come to the church and the Elders of the church will pray for me and anoint me with oil. I will be raised up and forgiven of my sins.

I didn't know any of this information. Church was new to me and so was all the protocol. I spoke in such a manner because I was hurting. I was hurting from my mom. It had only been 5 years since her death. I was hurting from not having a dad and also my situation with Gino. Gino had cheated on me in the past and was verbally abusive. This relationship was emotionally draining to me and Pastor Jackson could see that. It was difficult for me to hear and receive it from him because I never had to listen to any man. I didn't have a real relationship with a father and never had to respect any man of authority because I literally never witnessed it.

All of this was foreign to me. I didn't know where I really belonged. All I ever wanted was to be loved and accepted, but I have always guarded my heart in fear of rejection. It was becoming normal to me. My response was from a place of hurt and I needed peace. I knew deep down that Pastor Jackson was speaking the truth. He told me that Gino was not going to change and that he will continue to hurt me. I just didn't want to receive his warning and by 1994 I had left the church again. It was not totally based on Gino and my disobedience though. There were other factors that contributed to me leaving.

I was ecstatic to learn that the church had a dance ministry. So I joined the dance ministry and there was a lot of jealousy, envy and things going on to try and destroy me in that ministry. I believe it was because I had a dance background and the leader at that time was a bit insecure about that. I looked at that as an asset.

I could learn about worship and the spiritual aspect of praise in dance and they could learn about technique from me. I thought it would be the perfect combination. I was wrong. It was just three of us during that time and I guess I was the third wheel. It was horrible. It had been a while since I had danced. It got so bad, that one of the girls went to leadership and told how I was being treated. After the talk with our Co-Pastor, the dance leader came to me and tried to be more open and even offered her dance garments to dance on Sunday. I danced, but it wasn't the same. I realized that something that I was so excited about in the beginning was now tainted. The damage was already done. So I threw my hands up and left. Remember I was accustomed to running anyway so that's what I did.

I was very disappointed and hurt. I thought people in church were supposed to be nice and there was no need for competition. Boy was I mistaken. They were laughing at me during our prayer circle. This was before we went to the altar to dance. I literally opened my eyes and saw the young lady nudging the other girl and snickering while I prayed. There were times I was told that they didn't have anything for me to wear, so I couldn't dance. Also, having rehearsals without me. Finally, I said. I might as well have stayed in the world. I know now that the house of God is a hospital and there are many there with issues. This young lady was being used by Satan and didn't even realize it. I was a babe in Christ and didn't understand *that* at the time. It was a lose lose situation and yet again, I was back in the world.

Gino and I had always talked about getting married. He had since moved out his mom's house and moved into a duplex. He asked me to move in and I refused to move in because I didn't think he was ready. Gino's place had turned into a party house. Every night was company; male and female and it bothered me. I was really torn during this time because I wanted to live right and live for God, but I couldn't let go of the life that I had been so accustomed to living. The man I loved was in the world. He was a party man. He loved the streets and in the beginning, we had so much in common because we loved the same things. We had so much fun, but something was shifting in me. I knew I was missing something and I needed God, but I couldn't find the balance. It was one extreme to the other.

When I was in church I was all about Jesus and going to service 3 days a week. I was telling everybody that they needed Jesus and was sending my family to hell. I was called a fanatic by my family and friends. I was definitely double minded. When I was in the world I was all about partying and sinning. On the other hand, with Gino everything was about partying. Life every day was about having fun. By this time, I had turned into inspector gadget. I snooped a great deal in this relationship. I found this receipt of two pagers that were bought. My name was written next to a number and the name Nika was also on the receipt next to a number.

I confronted him about the receipt. He admitted that it was the pager he had purchased for sweetest day. He explained there was a deal and his friend purchased another one for his girl. He said the purchases were made together to take advantage of the discount. I didn't buy it. "You're lying", I screamed. Tell me the truth because I am going to find out the truth anyway, so you may as well tell me the truth now. He called me crazy and denied that it was anything more. I told him please just tell me the truth. He went off on me for going through his stuff. He tried to flip the script. I knew that game too well. I begged him the entire day to tell me the truth but he didn't. We left and went to his friend's house. I asked him where does she live and he claimed he didn't know. I failed to mention to him that I had found something with her address on it. This was more confirmation that it was something more.

So, when we arrived at his friend's house. All his friends were there. I got out the car and started walking. I had on this cute two-piece mini-skort (skirt and short) set with my cute little black pumps. I started to walk. Yes, I did! I walked! Where the hell are you going? He asked. To Nika's house. All his boys fell out laughing. He laughed too. I kept walking. I walked about five blocks up and 2 blocks down. Searching for this girl's address. I arrived at her door. I knocked no answer. I knocked again, no answer. I knocked again, nothing. I turned to walk away, and then I heard the door slowly open. There stood this short girl, with big eyes. She actually favored me. I asked, "Are you Nika?" "Yes, I am," she replied. I asked if she knew Gino. There was this long pause.

She finally admitted that she knew Gino and that he had called her and told her that I may show up. He begged her not to open the door for me. He told her that I was his fiancé and that I had found an old receipt. Nika began to tell me details of her and Gino's relationship. How they dated for about three months and she later heard that he was in a relationship. That is when she broke it off. She asked to see my ring. I obliged. I had questions. I wasn't mad at her. It wasn't her fault; she was a victim of his lies also. I asked about Sweetest Day. Something in me just didn't believe his story about being arrested. I was right. She told me that Gino came over that night and watched movies with her and her mom. I thanked her for telling me the truth. She apologized for her part in my hurt. I left. I walked back with my mind made up. Heartbroken, I approached him.

"Are you satisfied now?" Did you get the answers you needed? Gino had no idea she opened the door. He still thought that he had that power to manipulate and control. "Yea I did! She told me everything!!! I clowned, yes I did. I called him every name in the book. It's OVER!!! I finalized that statement by taking off the diamond ring!!! I threw it!! The ring went flying over his friend's garage. Everybody screamed NOOOOOO….. Don't throw the ring! I didn't want it. It represented a lie. Gino was a cheater and a liar. I then left. He ran after me trying to get me to listen to him. I went home. I got on the bus and went home. Yes, from the eastside.

When I attended church, I remember learning about soul ties. I had never heard of that term before. A soul tie is when you are tied sexually and emotionally to someone. I was connected to him emotionally and spiritually through sex. The two become one through intimacy. This is how God designed it, to be a spiritual act. This is also why we are not supposed to have premarital sex, because God knows about the invisible yoke that comes with sex. The two of you become yoked together. In some cases, it can feel like bondage because you keep going back to something that is painful or dangerous. No doubt, I had a soul tie with Gino. That's why although he hurt me, I continued to go back over and over again. I couldn't shake this man. He was now a part of my DNA. I thought about him all the time. I loved him, I hated him and most of the time I prayed for him. I did.

I wanted him to be right. I wanted him to be the man that God called him to be. I often thought about the prophecies he received at Great Faith. I cared for him like he was my husband, but he was not. We were in fornication and not living the way God intended. He had so much potential, but refused to flee the devil. I felt so many different emotions, sometimes simultaneously! That's madness!! That's why God said. Don't fornicate, because it can cause all types of emotions and feelings that could end up being too overwhelming. These feelings can overtake you and even destroy you. Especially when you are tied to someone who is not your husband and who is not saved. I have since learned that having potential isn't enough. If a person is not committed to realizing that potential, potential is all they will ever have.

Although I had received Christ with my confession, I wasn't living holy. That was my battle. I battled with sexual sin and I needed deliverance. So I took another trip to the altar to break soul ties once again. I really believed I was done with Gino. Pastor Jackson asked me to come give my testimony on the Miracles Do Happen telecast but I refused. I gave him the excuse that I was afraid of the cameras. Me? Afraid? I knew deep in my heart that I still wanted to be with Gino. I could not allow myself to stand before God and those viewers and lie. So, I declined. Pastor tried to convince me that there were many young women out there in bad relationships and if they heard my testimony it may help someone. I told him that I would think about it. That interview never happened. Although, this relationship wasn't healthy for either of us, a couple of weeks of him begging me to come back wore my resistance again, although short-lived.

One HOT summer day Gino and I made plans to go to the movies and then hang out later. He was supposed to work on his car and his friend's car and then bring me some money. I waited all day for him to call me. No call though. Finally, I call him and he got me off the phone abruptly. "Baby I'm working. I'm trying to make some money!" I'll call you when I'm on my way. Another hour passed, so I caught the bus to his house. I was no longer working, so I was broke and he promised to bring me some money. As

I'm walking up the street, there is Gino. Shirt off, music blasting, dancing in the middle of the street. There are girls everywhere and his boys are encouraging him. "Go Gino, Go Gino" I walked up.

His boy went UT oh!!! Everything stopped. I went off, "So you have me waiting on you all day and you're out here dancing in the street." "You caught the bus over here?" "Yes, I caught the bus over here I need some money!!! We argue and the crowd begins to disperse. Gino's car was not finished and he asked his friend to drive us to his house. We argued the entire ride to his place. It was not pretty. We are sitting in his house and I am so upset I felt disrespected. Here he is again, with no regard for me and my feelings. I'm tired of this bullshit. I'm so tired of you. You are not the man for me. Everybody told me to leave your ass alone. I can't stand you.

So he says to me. You need to leave. Are you going to give me any money? No! I got mine. Where is yours? I got money. Gino pulls out some cash and flashes it. You got over here you need to get home. So, he takes me by the arm and slings me out of his house. I was beyond pissed. I could feel a rage rising up in me for everything that Gino had ever done to me. I walk to the side of his house. I see this brick lying on the ground. I pick up the brick and throw it through his dining room window. I took off running. I'm in a sundress with some mules with a French roll that Carol had put in my hair. I'm running down 94 service drive. Because I know Gino is coming.

Sure enough, here he comes running after me. There is a field, so I start to look for a weapon because I know this is about to be ugly. In the grass,

I see a 2 x 4 piece of wood with nails. I grabbed it. "Come on." I put the wood in swinging motion. I was going to bust his head to the white meat, if he hit me. I am Alice's Granddaughter. In my mind, I'm thinking he is about to kill me. "You are Crazy!!!" You crazy b@$%h!!! You are going to pay for that window. Gino looked down and saw my purse in the grass. He grabbed it and took my identification out. He then starts running back to his house. Now anyone with common sense would have tried to hitch a ride home or something. No, not me I went back to the house. While running from Gino I lost my shoe and I couldn't find it, so I had on one shoe. I get to the door and it's open. I could hear voices coming from inside. Gino was in the back at his neighbors. She lives in the duplex also. They share the laundry area and he was in her house. I never liked her and all I could hear was her saying you need to leave her alone she is crazy. So I start to confront her. "Oh I'm crazy huh?" Yeah let me show you how crazy I am. Gino grabs me and takes me back to his place. He threatens to call the police.

There is a hole in his dining room window the brick is on the floor. I really felt bad, but I was angry. Gino had done so many things to me over the years and I was really at my breaking point with him. He took the wood from me and told me that he had phoned the police. I said, "Ok cool, let the police come". I'm sure once they run your name and see that you owe back child support we both will be handcuffed. Gino turned beet red. GET OUT, GET OUT NOW!!! He takes me and pushes me out the door again.

I'm beating on his door and ringing his door bell. "Give me my purse I need my purse." I had one dollar in my purse and I needed to get home. At this point I didn't care. I needed my identification and my purse. Gino opens up the door and throws my purse out the door and then takes my pager that he bought me and throws it across Moross. It shatters in the middle of the street. Oh my God, I hate you!!! You lowdown dirty… I'm LIVID!!!! I take my shoe, turn it to the heel and went across the front room windows. BAP, BAP, BAP again. I broke the front 3 windows and took off running again. This time running for my life. I have seen Gino's temper and I knew he was going to beat me half to death. I ran and ran without stopping. Until I hear "Ms. Ms. are you running from that light-skinned man?" There were three little boys riding on their bikes. I was out of breath "Yes Oh my God… Where is he?" I answered. One of the children responded. "We told him that you went the other way, so that you could get away." I was so thankful. "Thank you so much!"

Listen, does any of you have any money? I need to get to a payphone." The children began to search their pockets and between the three of them, they gave me change to make a phone call. I knew that I had to get away immediately. I knew that if he caught me this time that he was going to seriously injure me. I had to think fast. I asked the children if I could get a ride. The one child told me to hop on the handle bars. I hopped on without missing a beat. So, within seconds, I'm riding down 94 service drive on the handle bars of this child's bike. His friends are trailing in behind us on their bikes. I could not believe it. This was unbelievable. This can't be my Life. How did it get to this?

I'm looking like I'm 12 years old with my shoe in my hand trying to hold on to this bike. My hair was literally standing straight up because that French roll was no longer a roll, but a point. I was dropped off at the McDonald's on Harper at the payphone. I thanked the children for the money and the ride. I made a call to my friend Carol and sat on the curb waiting for her arrival. Devastated, Disenchanted and Broken hearted. How could he treat me so badly? Is this really love? This can't be love. How did this beautiful summer day turn into a day of horror? I didn't have the answer.

I desperately needed to assess my life. I needed to make some changes. After the incident with the window, Gino came by that following week professing his love again. Talking about "Windows can be replaced, but you can't." I knew then, that he was just as crazy as I was. That soul tie was affecting us both. He wondered how I disappeared so quickly that infamous day. I reminded him of the little boys on the bikes. He was adamant that he never encountered or talked to any children on bikes that day. That seemed strange to me considering they stated there was an exchange of words. I believe God sent angels to give me a way of escape.

We were toxic and I had to stop the cycle. I told Gino that we had to stop hurting one another. He agreed and we decided to take it one day at a time. However, we both knew what that entailed. Gino had never been alone either. Once I found out that he was seeing other people, I started dating as well. Nothing serious though. I just needed a break from all the drama and chaos. Then the family also was notified that Charles, my brother's dad, had passed away. My brother didn't have a relationship with his father. He never tried to pursue a relationship with him either. I guess it was the best considering the circumstances. It had been years since any of us had any contact with him.

In retrospect it's puzzling, the women in my immediate family didn't drive. My Grandmother never learned how. My mother didn't drive or my Aunts. So, I was determined to get my license and a car. I went to Mel Far and of course I needed a cosigner and my Grandma did that for me. It was on and popping. I loved my little Red Shadow. All I had to do was make sure that I picked up my brother and cousin from school every day and picked up Grandma from work every night. I thought it was the perfect agreement in the beginning, but as they became teenagers. It was annoying. I was single and having fun. I had a car and I was beginning to believe things were turning around for me.

After two years of an in and out of a relationship with Gino, everything changed in fall 1995. Gino went to jail. Things changed really quickly because he needed a miracle. He and I were not in a relationship at this time, but we were friends. Gino was robbed and during the robbery, he shot the person. The guy did survive, but it was his word against Gino's. He was in the County Jail for 5 months. During this time, I was working for Focus Hope Manufacturing. I had gone through Machinist Training for a while. I came out the program and became employed there. Before work, I would go to church and pray at the altar for my family and for Gino. I did this faithfully. I even had some of my friends praying for him as well.

Don't misunderstand me, I knew Gino was a player, but he wasn't a murderer. He wouldn't maliciously kill anyone. He was charged with felonious assault with intent to commit murder. I didn't want him to go to jail. Deep down I still loved him. While in jail, he wrote me beautiful love letters and professed his love for me repeatedly. It was if being locked up and confined, gave him a revelation of God and me. He began to go to bible study there and read the Word. He would write me about God and I was very devoted to him. I waited for this moment for him to truly accept God and realize that he indeed had a call on his life. Sometimes I would go and sit on the steps of 1300 Beaubien or sit in my car just so he could see me. I know… I know… That was a bit dramatic and extreme, but I loved him and I was loyal and wanted him to know that.

He would put a white piece of paper in his hand and wave it, so I could see he was there. Gino vowed to do right by me. He pleaded for me to wait on him. He told me that he wanted to marry me. I believed every word he spoke. He even expressed to his mom that he wanted to marry me. She and I began to get close during this time. She saw how devoted I was to her son and loved the change in him. Well, during the trial. It didn't look good for him, but we prayed and believe God. His mom held my hand as the verdict was read. Gino was released. The guard told him "Man the God you serve is a miracle worker because people don't usually walk away from these charges." The day Gino was released I was very happy. We made plans to be together, we professed our love and devotion for one another. We even went to church together. During this time, we had moved from the little shack house on Lawrence to another flat on Calvert. My Aunt Bunnie's friend told my Grandmother that this guy named Jack owned the house and that we could move in. We were there about a month before there was a knock at the door and a man stated that he owned the home and not Jack. He had the deed and said that he had exchanged the house to Jack for some crack. There was no exchange of money or anything. So we had to move once again.

Gino and I decided to attend the church of a pastor who ministered to him and others while he was in jail. Gino loved the way he taught the Word. So I visited with him and things were good. My Grandmother then decided no more renting and decided to buy a house, she found a nice bungalow on the west side of Detroit. My Grandmother had worked overtime and saved her money to put a down payment on a home. We moved on Rutland on Christmas Eve 1995. Things seem to be finally coming together for our family. The house had a fenced in backyard, 3 bedrooms and a full basement. It was not long before I found out that I was pregnant.

Gino and I were both ecstatic. We didn't tell his mom right away because she was very disappointed in us. She believed that we were in sin and that we did not belong together. She eventually told Gino he couldn't stay with her anymore. So he asked my

Grandmother and she agreed that he could move in with me and my family. We were all so happy. Gino was welcomed with open arms. My cousin lived there too with his child's mother and their son. Along with my little cousins and my younger brother. I know this wasn't the ideal way of living, but that's how I grew up. My Grandmother opened her door to her children and their significant others and this was happening again in the next generation with me and my cousins.

Everything was fine. My baby was growing inside of me and I was getting bigger. Gino and I were closer than ever. He was working and I was still at Focus Hope. I was excited about going to my doctor appointments and taking my prenatal vitamins. Gino, me and the baby, were going to be a family! My immediate family was still apprehensive about Gino, but they wanted me to be happy. Gino was smooth. He tried his best to stay out of the way. He paid my Grandmother for staying there and drove her around to complete her errands when he could. I was just happy to be drama free. So I thought.

Gino's Mom would eventually come around to accepting our relationship. She wasn't pleased about how we got together and felt like we fell right back in to sin. She was correct, but it was our lives to live. We made mistakes over and over again. We both had choices in life and we had to live with those choices. She gave me some clothes she bought from the rummage sale and also sent some perfume to the house in an old bottle. Let's just say I never used that perfume. Gino thought it was a nice gesture.

Grandma didn't and told me to get rid of it. One day she invited us over to her house.

She was extremely nice this day and asked me how my pregnancy was going. I told her that everything was fine and that I should know the sex of the baby soon. I had an appointment for an ultrasound that week. She was cooking sausage and brought me some to eat. I told her that I wasn't hungry. My Grandmother had always stressed to me not to eat her cooking. My Grandmother was skeptical of her because of her ties to Louisiana and felt that she operated in witchcraft. I thought Grandma was being a bit paranoid because like I stated earlier, she and I were bonding, after Gino went to jail. So I started trusting her again. She took the plate back in the kitchen. Gino asked if he could have some, so she brought him his plate. "Baby this is good, you should try some" he stated. I looked at the sausage, it did smell good. "Okay" I said. But before I could reach for the sausage, his mom stops me. Noooo, don't eat his, that's for him. Yours is in the kitchen. She goes back in the kitchen and brings me back my plate. I eat and it was good.

The next day I could not get out of bed. I had chills and was burning up with fever. I went to the bathroom and something happened. My water broke. I was rushed to the hospital, examined by the doctor and was told I had a prolapse cord. The umbilical cord had detached itself from my baby and my baby could not receive nutrients or oxygen. I was told that my baby was no longer living. I was 5 months pregnant. I was heartbroken. My heart felt like it was being squeezed. I couldn't breathe. I laid there numb.

Gino asked the doctor what caused it. They couldn't tell him. Sometimes these things just happen they said. Because I was so far along. I couldn't have a D&C. I had to give birth to my baby. So I was given medication to induce my labor.

Gino's mother came to the hospital with Kentucky Fried Chicken and sat there and talked about how her daughter went through the same thing. My Aunt Allene came and comforted me because I wanted to curse her out and throw her out of my room. My Aunt looked me in my eyes and shook her head. To tell me don't do it. Gino's Mom said things such as, "It won't be long now" and "This is just how it was with Briana," that's Gino's sister. She treated this as if it was a normal birth. My baby was dead inside of me and she acted like it was a grand event. Finally, she left. It was Gino and I and our baby girl. Yes, she was a girl. I still had to give birth to her. She was stillborn. It was mentally and emotionally painful….

Afterwards my doctor came in and gave his condolences to us. He also explained that he believed I had an incompetent cervix. An incompetent cervix is a cervix that begins to dilate as the baby grows and gets bigger. The body tricks itself into thinking that it's ready for labor, the cervix dilates, which causes premature birth. The Doctor informed me that I could have a baby, but I would need a cerclage which is a stitch to keep the cervix intact. Gino was very upset. He was hurting, we both were. He told me that he didn't want to try anymore and maybe it was not meant for me to have children. I went into a deep depression. I also left my job because I wasn't sure really what caused my loss. I was hurt and confused.

Shortly after that, Gino was up to his old tricks again. I found out that he went to see the mother of his child that he denied. His claim was that her mom passed away and he wanted to give his condolences. It wasn't long before he was trying to sleep with her and I found out that there was a second child with her. This child was born during the time he lived in the duplex. Lie, Lies, and more Lies. I was fed up and wanted him out of my life.

I went and talked to Joseph, he was always my friend and confidant. I knew that he always loved me. He was my best friend. He was still attending Great Faith Ministries and was ushering at the time. After our visit, I kissed him. I don't know why I did. I was upset, hurt and also wanted to see if I would feel anything for this man that had always been there for me. He was surprised and so was I. I kissed him then I left and ran to my car. I broke up with Gino, told him that he needed to move out and I confessed to him about the kiss with Joseph. He was livid. He said. "I knew he wanted you; he is just trying to come between us." I reminded him that Joseph has always respected our relationship and that he was the one that constantly destroyed our relationship.

After deciding to break up with him. Gino, begged me to marry him. He argued that if we got married our issues would change. He professed that he'd be faithful and I would be more secure with our relationship. I told him I didn't believe that would change anything. I informed Joseph of his request. Joseph asked me to fast and pray before I married Gino. He told me that after fasting and praying if I still wanted to marry him, that he would give us his blessing. Like I stated earlier Gino was a charmer. He could be very persuasive when he wanted to be and he persuaded me to become his wife. I never fasted and prayed. We planned to get married on my birthday May 31, 1996.

My Grandmother and I went to Hamtramck and bought me a little white dress with a little white veil. Yes, I wore white… It was supposed to be just the two of us, but Gino told his mom. She insisted on driving to Toledo with us. I told my dad and he rode with us also. The day of my wedding, Grandma and I went to Dot and Etta's for shrimp; I was supposed to meet him at 12 noon. It was about 10 minutes after 12 and my Grandma said, "Are you sure you want to do this? You're supposed to meet him at noon, right?" I was very hesitant the day I married Gino. Deep down I knew I was making a mistake.

My heart wanted him to be right. My heart wanted it to be true, but so much had already happened. After a long pause. I answered Yes, I'm sure. We got married in front of the courthouse in Lucas County. My father is standing there angry. You see, that was his first-time meeting Gino face to face. My father was extremely upset with me. He knew that Gino and I had a history of problems, but my father's opinion didn't matter to me. Because he wasn't there in my mind to have an opinion. When was he there for me? So now you have an opinion. No, I didn't want to hear it. So we exchanged vows.

After we arrived home. We were greeted with hugs and well wishes from my family. They were excited for us. Later that evening we all met at the Sting nightclub after all it was my birthday. So we partied there. There was a cake and Gino and I kept our wedding attire on. I wore my little white wedding dress. Oh, by the way he wore white as well. We danced all night. I mean, we partied. That's what we always did. The next day my cousin treated us to dinner and we stayed at a hotel. About a week later my Grandmother gave us a wedding reception. Our family and friends came. We were happy. I realized that I was his wife and that we had finally overcome our obstacles.

Although, we were living in my Grandmother's house, we were now married. I thought everything was beginning to fall into place. I must admit I didn't know anything about being a wife. A wife, what was that? I didn't cook, because Grandma did the cooking. There was a lot I didn't comprehend about being a wife. I know I had a false idea about marriage. I believed it was supposed to be a fairytale. You know the stories we read as little girls about a Prince Charming sweeping you off of your feet. Today I realize that marriage is work and ministry. Two individuals, who need an equal exchange of love, commitment and communication. Gino and I were never great communicators. We argued. So, that didn't change. We continue to argue, have our disputes and the honeymoon was quickly over.

About six months into the marriage, Gino's mother sent me a letter. She accused me of trying to take her son away from her. I must admit, I didn't trust her. She came to our reception and stayed 10 minutes and was rude the entire time she was there. She came and saw the beautiful wedding cake that my God-mother Mrs. Blue bought me. The cake had real red roses on the border. She looked at the couple on top of the cake and pushed the face of the groom saying that the groom on the cake was too dark to be her son. I knew she didn't approve of our marriage. So, I did stay away to avoid drama. But I did go to her house to discuss the letter. We got into a huge dispute and she told me that she will always be first in his life.

I told her that it wasn't a competition. She quoted the bible to me saying, "Honor thy mother and thy father and thy days will be long." I quoted, "A man shall leave his father and mother and cleave to his wife." I told her that she needed to cut the umbilical cord. Gino was a mama's boy. I knew that going in, but she was worse than I imagined, calling constantly all day and night. I mean first thing in the morning. Sometimes 6 am. To 10 pm at night she called him. All throughout the day... There were no boundaries. I know it was not my place to set those boundaries, it was Gino's place, but she sent *me* the letter. We went back and forth.

Finally, we heard him come up the stairs. That's when she decided to give a performance. She begins to yell at me and say, "You are not first in his life. You are not first. You are his wife, but I am his mother. I come first!!!" Gino was very confused and upset and started yelling at me. "What are you doing? What have you done? He then ran out the house "Gino!!!" she yelled. She ran after him. I ran too. She reiterated, "She is not first in your life." "We are your family and when this marriage falls apart, because it will fall apart…. You are going to come back to us. Your family!" I tried to talk to him, but I could not get through. He believed that I had disrespected his Mom. That's exactly what she wanted him to think. She didn't start yelling until she heard him come up those stairs. It was a setup.

Gino, walked away from me. He wasn't hearing anything I had to say. He got in his car and drove away. I was waiting for him to say Mother, this is my wife. You have to respect her and the fact that I chose her. Baby this is my Mother. She will always be my Mother. You have to honor and get along with her. He didn't. That was too much like right, so he ran. That day I lost respect for him. He could have settled that whole situation. He could have made his voice heard in that moment. The manipulation would have ended that day. She wanted to put a wedge in our relationship and she did. The marriage was scorned. His mom cursed it that day. We went through the motions, but it was strained. This situation would be something he could use as a secret weapon in the future, something he could use to blame me for.

By winter 1997, we were attempting to move forward. I wasn't feeling quite myself, but he wanted to go to dinner. We went to Flaming Embers downtown to eat. As I sat there, he said to me you're pregnant. Why would you say that? I replied. He responded. "I know your body." I took a test the next day. I was indeed pregnant. That day when Gino came home I told him. He looked at me and said, "I guess I should hug you huh?" He hugged me and left. He went and sat in his car in the driveway. He sat out there for hours. I cried myself to sleep. I knew Gino didn't want me to be pregnant.

It wasn't that he no longer loved me, but I believe he was scared because of all the loss. He knew my history with pregnancies and couldn't understand why I didn't wait. I felt just the opposite. Because I suffered so much loss, I yearned for a child. I knew our love wasn't perfect, but I knew that we loved each other. What greater manifestation of that love. I wanted to have his child. So I went to the doctor. I started my prenatal care and I explained to the doctors that I had an incompetent cervix and needed the cerclage. They tested me and stated that my cervix was a bit short, but I probably didn't need a cerclage. I was in their high-risk clinic and that I would be monitored. I had to see the doctors weekly. Gino eventually came to accept my pregnancy.

It was an awkward time for us. He was working as a temp at Ameritech and seemed to really love the job. He got to dress in a shirt and tie every day and had a cubicle and computer at his desk. That job made him feel really important. I was against him working there because it was through a temporary agency. He was also called during that time to work at Focus Hope as a mechanic. I thought that job had more security and health benefits. I thought that job was more appropriate for someone who was married with a child on the way. He disagreed. He began to stay out late on Wednesdays. It was unusual. He told me that it was a class that he had to take for his job, so I didn't question it. I was working at the time at a temporary service. I was placed at a perfume company in Livonia. We boxed, UPC and shipped perfume to various department stores. The work wasn't strenuous and I met some amazing people there. Ms. Katharine was one person who I met and impacted my life.

She was in her 70's but looked about 30. She cursed like a sailor and was very funny. I also met a lady name Connie who was my supervisor in my section. She was Caucasian and funny too. She believed in the Lord, so we talked about God a lot. My other favorite person was Veronica. She was also a supervisor. She was all business, had a strong work ethic, but was also very nice. These women made my days at work. They were like a second family to me. They were all very concerned for me and looked out for me. I would talk to them about my marriage and my problems. They helped me because they were wives. I expressed my concern about Gino's Wednesday pattern, but they told me to focus on my baby. I had already named him Christian. So I focused on Christian. He was growing, getting bigger and stronger every day. I would leave work early every Friday and go to my appointments.

This one particular Friday, I was examined and the doctor said I had dilated. I was in disbelief. I didn't feel a cramp, nothing. I started screaming, "Put in the cerclage!!! Put in the cerclage!!! The doctor explained "It's too late. You have dilated 3 centimeters. You have to go straight to the hospital." So I had to call Gino and was transported to the hospital. Gino came.

The doctors informed me that I would have to stay the duration of my pregnancy in the hospital. They had my bed tilted and were giving me steroids to stop the labor. They were also giving me medication to help develop the baby's lungs. Gino was worried. He asked so many questions, his mom was there. I didn't mind. I needed all the support and love I could get.

My family and my friends came to see me too and my dad was even there. I had a lot of support. Everyone was worried about me. The doctors told me the truth! They didn't hold anything back. I had to stand on faith. Gino that night had plans to go see BB King. He loved his music and already had plans with his dad to go to the concert. He asked me would it be okay to go. I said no! I needed him there. He argued that his dad had spent a lot of money on the tickets and they shouldn't just go to waste. I gave in….

That night I felt really uncomfortable. I tossed and turned and couldn't rest. I was also upset that Gino went to that concert. Finally, I told the nurse I was a bit uncomfortable. So she checked me. "Oh my God!" You have dilated to 10. I'm so sorry I'm so sorry!!! She screamed. We have to take you now. I called Gino and told him. I'm crying and trying to stay calm. The next thing I know I'm being wheeled down the hospital hallway.

Now, they're scrubbing my stomach and informing me that I need an emergency Cesarean. I'm scared. It's just me and Jesus!!! I asked God to protect me and my baby. They put the anesthesia mask over my face and told me to count back from ten. 10,9,8,7… When I awakened, Grandma and Gino were there. Grandma said. He's tiny, but alive. Tears streamed down my face. The doctors informed us that it would be a long journey. Also, that he may have some developmental delays due to his prematurity. I was immediately overwhelmed, but grateful that my miracle baby was alive.

7.

Raising a Son with Autism

Christian was born on June 29, 1997. He was 24 weeks, 16 weeks premature, weighing 1 pound and 8 oz. I was told that he had a 1 out of 10 chance of survival, but I knew he was that 1. After I was released from the hospital, things changed quickly. Gino and I had to grow up. No more petty arguments and living with Grandma. Reality kicked in. We were parents to a child that needed all of our attention, energy and love. One night, things got really bad. We had a very heated argument and he called me a b@#$h. So again, I was not going to take that lightly. So I called his mama a b@#$h. So he came back even harder than that and said. Your Aids infected mama is a b@#$h. That was it!!! I screamed… No you didn't No you didn't! My Grandma heard me screaming and said. "What the hell is going on now? Y'all are the last motherf@#&ers on earth that should have ever gotten married." She screamed. I told her what Gino said. I probably shouldn't have, but I was enraged! Next thing you know my Grandma had grabbed her hammer and called all my cousins and my brother. Gino was getting put out the house. He's staring at me like, Are you really letting them put me out? I didn't say a word. I was numb. My male cousins start grabbing his clothes and throwing them on the grass. Before I knew it, Gino was gone and I was devastated. My family declared that he could never come back and that he was no longer welcome there. Within an instant, our lives had changed forever.

My husband was gone. It all happened so fast and I had no control of the situation. We eventually talked the next day and he told me that he was living with his sister. He apologized for the rude statements that he made. Those words were unforgivable. I wasn't ready to forgive him. I had to focus on my son. Eventually Gino and I forgave one another for the verbal exchange that occurred that night. We had to put aside our differences to focus on our son.

Christian stayed in the hospital for 3 months. During that time, Gino and I saw one another after work. Sometimes we would meet at the hospital and meet for dinner on weekends. We would go to the hotels to spend quality time together. It was never enough time; we were disconnected physically which had an impact on our emotional attachment. The both of us knew that he was no longer welcomed at my grandmother's and we needed a place of our own. We were trying to reconcile and bring our family together. There was a lot to prepare for. Neither one of us was prepared for our son to have these challenges. There was a deep strain on the marriage and I was drained emotionally. I returned to work shortly after having Christian because we needed money. We were trying to save for us to be reunited as a family. I had the keys to our new apartment days before his release. I was ecstatic and scared at the same time. It was a new beginning for our lives. Gino and I finally had a place of our own and our son was coming home. I was given tons of information regarding his arrival home and I was tremendously overwhelmed. It was hard on us. I knew this was not an ideal situation and in order for us to have a chance, we actually needed a new start.

There was too much influence from both of our families. Gino's family didn't like me at all and my family was accustomed to being in each other's business. My brother, cousins and Grandma only wanted the best for me and felt that Gino fell short. Everyone hoped that the birth of Christian would mature the both of us. I often thought back to the warning of Bishop that he was not my husband. At this time, I was determined to prove everyone wrong. Always listen to the Man of God that has been placed in your life. He has insight.

Upon Christian's departure from the hospital, there was a meeting. A team of doctors met with Gino and I, to explain the seriousness of his illness and care. They needed for us to be ready for our new journey as parents to a child that has special needs. I was trained in CPR in case he ever stopped breathing. It was very scary, but necessary. Finally, Chris came home. I was so excited!!! I never had a baby shower because he was born so early. I gave myself a shower, a couple of days before his arrival home. The guest list consisted of family and a few close friends came. I felt so lost though. Those were the longest 3 months of my life. I experienced so many emotions during that time. I felt empty because I knew my baby was lying in a hospital. I would go to the NICU and lay his little body on my chest. The doctors encouraged this because they said he needed to feel the warmth of my body and hear my heartbeat. Normally at 25 to 30 weeks babies are still in their mother's womb. They wanted him to feel my warmth and comfort. Some days I would be alone. Some days Gino would go and some days we would go together. My baby was fighting for his life, and I was fighting for my marriage and my mind.

I had all kinds of questions. Lord, why did this happen to me? I wanted a child so bad and yet I have loss two. The devil also reminded me constantly of the pregnancy I terminated and I carried the guilt and the shame of that with me. Here I was, 27 years old with a baby, who I carried and love. He was so weak and so fragile... Yet so strong. Why??? God Why?? I wish that I could take his place. He was innocent. Why did he have to endure being poked with needles and be hooked up to all kinds of tubes and machines? Yes, I did question The Father? I was the one that was in sin. I was the one that did wrong! I was the one that sowed seeds of fornication!!! Punish me Lord! Don't allow my child to go through this. It was during this time that Christian's father expressed his desire to end the marriage. I believe it was partially because he had difficulty coping with Christian's medical condition.

In the beginning, it was a struggle for us financially. As a result of Christian's pre-maturity and medical condition, I couldn't work because he needed 24-hour care. When I attempted to work, employment was limited because he had seizures. Fortunately, my family was extremely supportive and my Grandmother was there for me. There were many days I cried out asking the Lord how I was going to do this. I had never experienced anything like this in my entire life. I had no prior knowledge to reflect back on regarding mental impairments or children with special needs. I was lost and didn't know where to turn for support. So I relied on the medical experts to guide me through this transition.

As Christian developed, there were several statements made by physicians telling me that he would never walk, and that he may have hydrocephalus (*fluid on the brain*) that will require a shunt in his brain. Every time I was given a negative report, I would lay hands on my child and declare healing in the Name of Jesus and not receive their prognosis. When he was first born, he had a hole in his heart. He was scheduled for surgery and everything. Right before surgery, they checked again and the hole was closed. Praise God!

Although, I backslid and was in and out of church, I still recalled Bishop's messages on faith and standing on the Word of God. The scriptures state that God is married to the backslider and He still honored my prayers. I thank God for the foundation that Bishop Wayne T. Jackson and Dr. Beverly sowed into my life. Applying God's principles of faith were new to me, but it worked and I praised

God and was thankful. Every test came back negative. Finally, at the age of two, still non-verbal and low functioning cognitively, Christian was diagnosed with cerebral palsy and further tests indicated that he displayed characteristics of Autism. By this time Gino and I had separated and he was living with the woman that he had the affair with. Well, this is how I found out.

We had just moved into our apartment. We were there about three weeks and I could tell Gino was adjusting to the situation, but I couldn't focus on him. I had to focus on my little baby. He would come home and complain about the house and dishes in the sink. I was very overwhelmed and depressed. Because all he did was complain. Finally, one day he comes home with a brand-new car. There was no discussion or anything about purchasing a new vehicle. "Hey baby this is the family car." This car was far from a family car. It was a Jaguar. I thought it was a bit irresponsible to buy a car and have a note with a new baby. Let's go for a ride. I had an attitude, but went.

All of sudden Christian starts vomiting in the car and Gino almost had a heart attack. I thought it was hilarious. I figured Christian even knew that was ludicrous. A week later, a friend of mine came to visit. I left the baby on the bed and asked Gino to keep him while I take her home. I was gone about 30 minutes. When I arrived home, Christian was still in the same spot. He didn't even pick him up. Chris had an apnea monitor and had leads on his chest. That machine would beep if he stopped breathing. There were times when that machine would beep in the middle of the night. It was extremely stressful. Gino tells me that he didn't move Chris because he didn't want the machine to beep. I wasn't buying it. I wrote him a letter telling him how much I wanted our marriage to work. I knew that it was an adjustment, but we both had to step up. I reminded him how hard we fought to get to this moment and was finally a family. He politely told me that he didn't want to be married anymore. "What do you mean you don't want to be married anymore?" I asked. He repeated it. We started to argue. I was hurt and confused.

He asked me what happen the day that his mother and I had that argument. That happened over a year ago!! But apparently, Gino never got over it. So, I explained again what happened. We argued some more. He explained that he hated our apartment. That it was too small and congested. He also expressed his dislike of the neighborhood. I admit, it wasn't the best apartment, but it was close to my grandma. He said that he would move out. I asked him about the rent because I had left my job to take care of Christian. He replied. That he had to pay his car note and that he couldn't pay the rent.

I was devastated. He went to bed and we didn't speak anymore. The next day he called me from work. The conversation was vague and dry. I felt as if I was in the twilight zone. I could not believe what had transpired. Three weeks after our son comes home. He wants to end our marriage. So, I went to my faith. I built an altar in my house. I lit candles and had my bible and scriptures everywhere. My friend Carol came by and thought I had lost my mind. Maybe I had. I just knew that I needed to anchor myself in God! I couldn't focus on Gino. My child needed me. The next day Christian's nurse came by and said that she didn't like his color. She also said he seemed a bit lethargic. She suggested that I take him through emergency. The doctors decided to admit him for observation. Gino came after work and checked on him and left. We didn't discuss anything. While at the hospital Christian stopped breathing. I remember screaming and the doctors came and took him out of my arms. The sirens for code blue were ringing. They took him and ran into a room. I wasn't allowed to go in. I cried, I screamed and I prayed. I asked God to spare his life. I asked God to save him.

The hospital sent a chaplain up to sit and pray with me. Finally, after about 10 minutes. Someone came and said that they had to get Christian to breathe again. It was just too much. I was there alone and it was too much. I asked to use the phone to call Gino. He asked was Christian breathing. I replied, "Yes, he's breathing. Are you coming back to the hospital?" "No, I'm not coming back." "Somebody has to go to work tomorrow!" I hung up the phone and sobbed. I cried for myself, I cried for my baby. My heart was broken in to a million pieces. They kept Christian for about three days for observation.

While he was in the hospital. Gino stayed out one night. He just didn't come home, I paged him. He didn't respond. I knew that our marriage was over. I started looking through all of our pictures and started ripping them up. The phone rang. It was my Grandma. "Did Gino come home last night?" she asked? "No, he didn't." I answered. "I didn't raise you to be treated like this!" She replied. You need to come home. There was silence. She repeated. "Do you hear me?" "I did not raise you to be treated like this." I'm sending the guys around to get your stuff. You and the baby's clothing. Just come home. You have a family who will take care of you and Christian. I said Ok and hung up the phone.

Gino came home that morning; He lied and said that he fell asleep at his sister's house. I told him when my husband starts spending nights out that the marriage is clearly over. He didn't say a word. He saw the ripped pictures on the floor and puts his head down. I told him my plans to leave. He said that he would be out by the end of the week. I left that night. Two weeks later I found out after pursuing child support that Gino's Jaguar was not in his name. I needed the plate for his car and the tabs didn't match his birthday.

Through some investigating, I found out the woman's name that the car was registered in. I also found out how much the loan was for and the amount of the car note, $315.00. Her work number and her address. So, I called her. I found out that Gino had been in an affair with this woman for over a year. I spoke to her on the phone and she confirmed everything. She knew about me. She knew about the baby. She knew so much because this woman was actually his boss. His supervisor. They would meet after work on Wednesdays. Apparently, the affair started after he confided in her about our problems and she would give him advice. When he was escorted out of my Grandma's house that night, he just moved in with her. They were already involved.

He never stayed with his sister, it was all lies. I filed for divorce in January of 1998. My heart was broken. Here I was with a baby that was ill and my husband decides to leave me to shack with his mistress.

Sylvia was very manipulative, cunning and very smart. She talked to me frequently, mostly to get me to express how I felt. She then would run back to Gino and tell him everything I said. I blamed them both. I blamed him because he was my husband and had vowed to be faithful and honor me. I placed my life in his hands and he dishonored me. I blamed Sylvia because she was fully aware that he was married. She was also older, and from my understanding, married herself. Sylvia was about 20 years older than Gino. She had experience, resources and she was his boss. She held the cards and she played the game well. We were both pawns in her hands. She played girlfriend with me. "Girl He did what?" I admit I was naïve. I shared our history with her and she used every word to manipulate the situation. Everything I told her she exaggerated it and Gino and I fell further and further apart.

Sylvia lived in a big beautiful home. No wonder Gino complained about the apartment being too small. He had been living in a nice, plush, Colonial house. She had job security and was financially stable. She would take Gino on trips and lavish him with clothes. She bought him Coogie sweaters, gator shoes and expensive jewelry. She even bought him a mink coat. I guess you could say she was his Sugar Mama. I would call him for diapers and things of that nature and Sylvia didn't like it. She told Gino to inform me not to call the house. I had to page him or call his cell phone. Although Gino was living with this woman. He would still call me every morning when he got to work.

He would tell me that he still loved me and he would say that he didn't want a divorce. I was torn and it was a very difficult and confusing time. I knew that he was a dog. I knew that he was a liar, but I still loved him. I believe, me never having a dad in the home, played a humongous role in this behavior. I never had a family with a mother and father together and I yearned for that stability. I wanted to offer that to my son, so I listened to him and believed him. My friends and family were very disappointed in me. Well, I was disappointed in me. I truly wanted my son to have his father in his life. Even if it was based on a LIE. It was then that my faith began to waiver.

I was on an emotional roller coaster. I would periodically visit the church. I was basically in and out during this time and no longer going regularly. I repented to Bishop Jackson for not heeding his warning. I needed to heal because I was not only dealing with hurt and betrayal, but I had a little innocent baby in the equation. Mother Dalton had counseling sessions. So I requested to see her. She told me that witchcraft was used to break up my marriage. I didn't know what to believe. All I knew was that one day I was married and within months, everything was destroyed.

Watching my child struggle with mental, social and communication skills was heartbreaking. I went back and forth with belief and unbelief. It was if someone had died and I was in mourning. All of the dreams and plans for my son's life in my eyes had vanished. Dreams such as his graduation from high school, attending college, getting married or myself ever becoming a grandmother were gone. I cried for all those dreams a parent has after nurturing and raising a child. Deep in my heart I knew that God would make a way out of no way, but I was too emotionally and physically drained to see how.

I was in a lot of turmoil. I was hurting; I just didn't understand why everyone that I loved, I lost. It felt like I was cursed! It felt as if I was doomed for failure and sadness. I was literally fighting for my life and mental stability. I lived with my grandmother and my family, but I knew that I needed my own space. It was time for me to grow up, I needed to mature. I knew that I had my family's support, but I couldn't continue to be this little girl, who depended on the safety net of her family. It was time to be a woman and make things happen for myself. So I wanted to get our own place again. I was receiving money from the state of Michigan. I was a single mother with a child with special needs. I didn't want to go to the State of Michigan for assistance, but I had too.

I didn't have a husband to provide for us. He had left. These programs are designed to assist you and help families get back on their feet. I was thankful and grateful for the financial assistance and I also received food stamps. I had always worked since I was 14 years old, but life happened and I was put in a position where I needed financial and medical assistance. We also qualified for WIC, Women Infants and Children. This program provided nutrition for me and my son. We were eligible for milk, eggs, cheese, and cereal. Because Christian was premature he needed a special prescription for his milk. WIC honored that request. Christian was receiving Social Security for his disability. It was hard, but we were surviving. A lot of people abuse the system, but it's there to help those that are in need and we were definitely in need.

I had taken Gino to court for child support. He was obviously upset about it, but I didn't care about his temper tantrum. He even pretended to want to reconcile with me in order to get out of paying. He called the Friday before our court date, which was on a Monday and asked me not to go to court. I laughed. He was so predictable. He then asked me if I was going to church that Sunday. I told him that I was. Gino comes to church that Sunday. He sat there during service and I'm sure felt very convicted when the Word came forth. During altar call, he goes to the altar. He begins to cry and run from one side of the altar to the other. I wasn't sure if he was giving his life to Christ or giving us a mime performance. Yeah right!

Of course, it was a performance because court was in the morning! Gino was escorted to the back for prayer. He came out to look for me and the baby. He found us in the back of the sanctuary. He looks at me and said. "My Family." I wasn't impressed. I knew he was playing a very deceitful game. He did it before when I first got saved. Don't play with God. Gino was not sincere. He had been given warning after warning by the man of God about his life and he didn't listen. Here he was playing again. He walked us to the car and left. Monday Gino was not at the child support hearing and he was ordered to pay.

A few months passed and I had moved out of Grandma's and was living in a four-family flat. My friends Carol and Monique were already living in the building. So I felt comfortable. It felt good to be on my own and have my own place again. We were in the process of the divorce and I was eligible for the lowest package based on my income. Michigan is a No fault state, so my attorney wasn't interested in anything pertaining to adultery or cheating. None of that mattered to him. It was pretty cut and dry. Gino was served on his job. There were times when I doubted my decision. Those were the times he would call and once even told me he wanted to try and save the marriage and go to counseling. I eventually knew it was another lie. I honestly believe he just didn't want to pay child support. I wanted to focus on me and my son.

The day of our divorce, I went to court and he wasn't present. I knew he wasn't going to show up. It was officially over. Later that afternoon I saw him on the Lodge service drive. Carol and I were in the car and Christian was in the back seat. He looked over at us and didn't say a word. He then turned his head as we sat at the light. Carol went ballistic. Are you kidding me? You mean to tell me he isn't going to acknowledge you? It's okay. I said. It doesn't matter anymore. My eyes began to tear up. Miki y'all baby is in the car. He ignored Christian. He could have blown the horn waved or something. I can't stand him. I feel like grabbing this club and beating his ass. Again, I repeated. It's okay. Tears began to fall down my face. I tried to pretend that it didn't hurt me, but it did. I had been with Gino for 5 years. He asked me to marry him promising to love me and here he was in the lane next to me treating me like a stranger. Carol knew that I was hurt. We both had been through a lot and had become really good friends. "That's okay girl, we are going to celebrate tonight!"

I had plans to go out and celebrate at Chucks Millionaires that night. I invited a few of my friends to party with me. I wore this cream crepe pant suit with a façade and a mask because I acted that night. I should have won an academy award for that performance. I hollered it's over! I'm a free woman now. I stayed on the dance floor all night drinking, partying, laughing and masking all of my pain. I was in pain. My heart ached. The night of my divorce. I almost lost my life. I was anxious about the court date so I had not been sleeping for days. On the way home, I fell asleep at the wheel. I woke up right before crashing into a parked car. It was a warning…

When I arrived home, Shellie had been calling me all night. "Girl are you alright?" I have been interceding for you, all night long. I told her well your prayers just saved my life. I told her what happened earlier in the day when I saw Gino on the street. I knew I was spiraling out of control. I could have died. My Grandmother had my son for the night and the next day I went to her house and told her what happened. We sat at the kitchen table and I confessed to her. My Grandmother is a strong woman, is she perfect? No! But she has always had the ability to get me straight! She was very upset with me. "So today your son could be without his mother?" Miki, you have to get it together. I know that you are hurt, but this little boy needs you. You are not the first woman whose husband has cheated and left and you will not be the last. Let him go!!! Then, it happened. I broke down and cried! I sobbed like a baby. I needed to release it. I was tired of masking and pretending I was okay. He left me and our son. She was absolutely right, He wasn't worth it. It was time for me to take care of my son. I had to stop hanging in those bars and I needed to be a mother. A real mother, who puts her child first. So the first thing I did was enrolled back in school and looked for a job.

I registered in two classes at Wayne County Community College. Everything was going well then, my car broke down. Then right after that my Grandma Belle, my dad's mother was diagnosed with breast cancer. She never complained and praised God all the way through, until she took her last breath. I had never seen that before. She would say things such as I love you Lord. I thank you Lord. Lord you're Holy. All through her suffering she praised God. She was truly a woman of faith. I know that she is with the Lord and rejoicing with the angels. My heart was broken for my dad and my Granddaddy because He loved my Grandma so much. She was the glue that kept the family together. Rest in peace Grandma Belle.

I started working at Dot's part-time and it was exciting to be able to work again. Grandma watched Christian for me so that I could work. She was the only person I trusted with my son. I was so enthusiastic about this job because it was nice to be amongst people again. I have always been a people person. I love to interact and talk to people. My boss absolutely loved me because I came in there ready to work, ready to learn and ready to advance. So I was catching the bus and getting rides to work and the blizzard of 1999 hit that year. It was terrible. I remember catching the bus to Telegraph and walking down to Chicago in the snow. Sometimes I would get to work with icicles on my eyelashes. I was very determined to make a life for me and my son. I worked extra hours, came in on days off and made employee of the month for 3 months straight.

My boss Joyce was very gracious and kind to me. She was married and had children. She saw my potential and really encouraged me. I remember her saying one day, "Ramona, I can't wait for everything to work out for you! You are such a good person." That meant a lot to me because most of my life I had been misunderstood. So for her to say that, really meant something. I knew that I was a good person. I have always been. Most times it's been difficult to convey that because I've been hurt a great deal. Therefore, I protected myself and appeared guarded and often unapproachable.

After a few months, I was transferred to the Grandland store and promoted to an Assistant Manager. I didn't want to transfer, but they needed help there. I was very dissatisfied at that store. The morale was down and the work ethic just wasn't the same from management. I knew that I would not be able to thrive in that environment. I immediately started looking for another job. Although, Gino and

I were divorced, he still was calling and coming by. I had become the other woman. I don't know why I allowed him to treat me like that. My self-esteem was gone. I was dating casually, but nothing serious. I'm sure you're thinking why are you dating? I was dating because I felt so rejected. I do have to clarify. I had male friends. I've always had male friends. Now I'm not saying that some of these friends didn't like me. I'm saying that there were a couple of men in my life who were strictly friends.

We would go to dinner or go to the movies. These friends I valued and they were truly there for me and supportive. I think it's important to have male friends because they give you a man's perspective. My friends gave me insight on the male's thought process and even their actions. My father was more prevalent in my life at this time because I had Christian and he adored his grandson. He'd try and give me advice about men, but it was difficult for me to listen and receive anything from him. I still had abandonment issues.

I decided to confront him about those issues. He didn't handle it very well. I asked him if he denied me as a baby. Of course, he denied it and accused my mother and grandmother of lying to me. He appeared to be very hurt by the accusations, but refused to look at me. I knew then, that there was some truth to the story. I admitted to him that my life would have been so much better if he had been a part of it. I expressed to him how much I needed his love and how his absence and rejection altered my life. My father couldn't handle the conversation and walked out. He stated that I wasn't listening to him. He later returned, but nothing was resolved. It all was swept under the rug. We both pretended that everything was fine. I believe my father wasn't ready to face his demons. All I really wanted from him was reassurance and an apology. I never received it. It was obvious that he wanted to forget the past and micro manage my love life and that wasn't happening.

Sometimes, I would go to a movie or meet someone at a party, but I was not intimate with them. I still believed Gino was going to come back to me. Sometimes I would ride pass the house with Chris in the back seat. I didn't understand how he could sleep at night. Even though we had divorced, I was still hoping to bring my family back together. My son had his challenges and I was trying to be the best mother that I could be. But there were times I was lonely and wanted to be loved. I had my friends, who were trying to uplift me and be there for me, but I wanted and missed the companionship of a man. So when Gino would call and ask to see me I would allow it.

Sometimes he would bring a movie and stay for a couple of hours. There were times that we were intimate and in my mind, I thought he still loved me. Then one night everything changed. Gino came by and we made love, well at least I did. Afterwards we were lying in bed and talking and I decided to ask a question that I had never asked before. Do you love her? Do you really love her? I asked again. "Yes I do," he replied. There was a long pause. I was flabbergasted. "I thought you were only with her because of what she could do for you?" Gino told me that he did love Sylvia. I argued "But she is 20 years older than you? And if you love her so much why the hell are you in my bed?" I began to get upset. Gino then gets up and puts on his clothes. "Here you go!" Why are you here? I demanded to know. I needed to hear him say it. Just tell me the truth I begged. Finally, he said I'm here because the sex is good! I was crushed, I told Gino to leave…. he walked to the door stood in the doorway and explained that he did love me, and that he loved Sylvia too.

At that point, I was exhausted mentally and emotionally. I shut the door behind him. Christian and I were residing in Cass Corridor during this time. I had often heard horror stories about Cass Corridor. That it was a part of the city full of homeless people and poverty. So, my Grandmother was terrified of us moving to the apartment. This apartment was really nice. They had renovated a historical building off Cass and Brainard. I applied for this one-bedroom low income apartment. The building was renovated and it had secure gated parking, cameras upon entrance and everything. The rent was 300.00 a month with gas included and everything was updated. It had a dishwasher, stove, microwave, garbage disposal and refrigerator included. It had and updated bathroom with ceramic tile and beautiful cathedral ceilings. I loved my little apartment. I was so happy when I first moved in, but the peace was starting to leave.

Then there was Leon. I met him at the gas station. He flirted with me from the time I walked in, to the time I walked out. He repeatedly asked for my number. I finally gave in. We talked on the phone the next day. He wanted to take me to the movies that following Friday, but I already had plans to go out that night to a birthday party. As I was leaving the party he called and we met near the river behind the Post Office downtown. He was cool, laid back and he seemed really sweet. He cracked a lot of jokes and was interesting to talk too. He was tall, handsome and it was obvious he stayed in the gym. He worked for Chrysler, had no children and had never been married.

We went on a few dates. It was hard to schedule dates because of his schedule at work. He worked a lot. Sometimes he would stop by after work with his bottle of cognac and just talk. He served in the military during the Gulf war in the 90's. He would jump on the counter in my kitchen and talk about his experiences there. It sometimes scared me because he would go to a dark place and I would have to bring him out of it. Anyway, this one particular night, Leon came by and he and I had a couple of drinks. Things begin to get a little hot and heavy and we had sex. Afterwards we laid there for a moment talking and laughing and enjoying each other.

All of a sudden Leon begins to aggressively kiss me again. I said, "No I am done." He replied. Come on, I want to do it again. I repeated. No, I'm done. I don't want too. I see a rage in his eyes and he says, "B@#$h, we just did it and I'm not done yet." He then flips me over. I'm fighting him and telling him to get off of me. "Get off of me Leon". "What are you doing?" He pins me down and proceeds to enter me from behind. "Stop, Stop" I screamed. I don't want to have sex. Vaginal sex was not what he was after this time, at this point Leon is inside of my rectum and I'm in disbelief and shock. He then gets up. I'm lying their numb with tears streaming down my cheeks. Get out!! Get out!!! I shouted.

Leon gets up like nothing happens. He puts on his clothes and he leaves. I couldn't believe what had just happened. I was really confused about it because. This was a man that I was dating and this was our first sexual experience. I consented to the vaginal sex, but I didn't consent to the anal part of it. I was confused about what happened. Was it my fault? Did I bring this violation on myself? I was full of shame and anger at the same time.

Leon called repeatedly, but I didn't answer the phone. This went on for about a week. I went into a depression. I wouldn't talk to anyone. My friends were calling and I avoided everyone. I felt so ashamed and embarrassed. I was embarrassed because this violated me, yet I had consented for him to be in my home. How could I have been so naïve, so stupid and so desperate? I blamed myself. I felt shame and condemnation for my actions.

Finally, my friend Joseph called, "What is going on with you?" Something isn't right with you!" I blurted out "Leon raped me." That was the first time that I actually said it. "Leon raped me!!!! I informed Joseph the details of the encounter. He was furious!!! He was also upset with me that I didn't call the police. I tried to explain to him that I was confused about what actually happened because I did have sex with him. This man was invited to my place and we were drinking. I explained that it would be hard to prove. Joseph finally understood my dilemma and offers to have him beat up. I seriously just wanted to never lay eyes on him again. After two weeks passed, Leon called again. I answered the phone.

"Hey, I've been calling you. I have an article that I want to send you on Autism. Didn't you say that your child may have autism? I hung up the phone. He calls back and I confronted him about what he did to me. He then replies, "What are you talking about? "I didn't consent to anal sex Leon you raped me." He laughed, I raped you? Girl you are crazy!!! Look, good luck with your son, I will send the article. He hangs up the phone. I didn't pursue any charges and I never heard from him again. Oh, and he had the nerve to send the article.

Love Nots

8.

Creepin' with the Deacon

It was August 1999 and I had gotten a job as a teller at Comerica bank. I was really trying to move on with my life. Christian was 2 years old and there was therapy, after therapy and endless doctor appointments. I decided to get a job part-time to have some extra income. My Grandmother was gracious enough to watch Chris while I went to work. I was also still attending Wayne County Community College part-time. My life was beginning to feel normal again. One Friday afternoon the bank was packed. Fridays were always busy and we were always prepared for the rush. This guy was in line and yes, I noticed him because he was fine.

He approached my window. I asked for his identification and cashed his check. I noticed that he worked for Chrysler. He looked at me and I could tell that he was flirting. I wasn't there for that though. Many guys would come to my window and flirt, but after all my drama. Men were the last thing on my mind. So, as I'm counting the gentleman's money.

He keeps staring. I ignore him. Finally, he asked was I married. I answered. No. He asked why not? I replied, "Because I did not want to be unequally yoked." He then asked, "What church do you go to?" I responded, "What makes you think I go to church?" Because you used the words unequally yoked. Most women don't use those words. I didn't respond. I handed him his envelope and told him to have a good day. Betty the girl that worked next to me said, "Girl why didn't you get his number?" He was definitely flirting with you? I said, "If it was meant to be that he would be back." She thought I was crazy. Girl He was fine. You should have given him your number. I laughed.

The following week he was back. Once again there was a line. He allowed other customers to go ahead of him so that I could assist him. Then he got to my window with those beautiful brown eyes. Betty looked over at me and said, "I guess it's meant to be." I ignored her. Dion and I exchanged numbers. He told me he would call me. I wasn't impressed. I was actually tired and fed up at this point. I had been through so much. So, when I met Dion I felt this guy was someone I could date for real.

He called me on his lunch break that same evening. He told me that he was saved and in the church. He explained that he was a deacon in training and that he was looking for a wife. I thought oh my God, he's saved. He is in the church, that was all I heard. Remember, I was hoping to meet someone who loved God as much as I did. This guy seemed to be perfect. There was one thing that someone would think was not perfect, but I really thought it made

Dion the perfect man for me. Dion had a speech impediment. He stuttered really badly. I mean, there were times it was a real struggle for him to get out complete sentences. I'm not exaggerating. I thought he was perfect and I believed God sent him to Chris and me. Chris was nonverbal and I wanted a father for him who would understand his disability.

Dion was like someone out of a storybook. He literally swept me off my feet. We talked every day. He worked midnights but he would call often. We met for lunch and really seem to have the same values. He was very adamant about me not talking about Gino. He called him a loser and told me that Christian and I deserved better. The only thing that bothered me about Dion was that he seemed to be a bit materialistic. I remember one day he came to my job on my lunch break. I had some slide in shoes on. He broke out and said. I hate your shoes. What? I said. He repeated that he hated my shoes. He said that my shoes looked cheap and asked where I bought them. I told him Payless. "Girl, why are you wearing Payless shoes?" Shoes are shoes it doesn't matter I responded. I was offended. I got out of his truck and went inside.

The next day he was back and brought me a bouquet of red roses to my job. My boss was so excited! Oooou, he gave you red flowers. Red means love. Girl, does he love you? Maybe he loves you. Love was the furthest thing from my mind. I merely saw Dion as someone who could possibly be my soul mate. I wouldn't dare utter those words to him because I had been through too much hurt. Then one night everything changed. Dion came by. He came through the door with an Elmo doll for Christian. Christian loved Elmo and I had mentioned it to Dion. Christian was with Grandma, she baby sat him so that I could have some free time. I cooked dinner and we listened to music. He liked old school like me. We listened to the Isley Brothers and the O'Jays. We even danced. He could dance a little bit. Mostly, we talked for hours. He told me that he was looking for a wife. That wasn't the first time that he mentioned that. He told me that he really enjoyed spending time with me and Christian and by February I would have a ring.

Tears streamed down my face. He told me that he was falling in love with me and that he absolutely adored my son. He told me that Gino was an idiot and that another man's trash is another man's treasure. Things got a little hot and heavy that night. I realized there were still some real men out here. Gino??? I was like Gino who??? Who Dat?? Dion and I were getting closer.

One morning Gino called asking to come by. I told him that I was seeing someone and that I was happy. He was sarcastic as usual. I didn't even care. It felt good to be with someone who knew what he wanted, who loved God and cared for my son. I hung up on Gino! As time passed, Dion and I got closer and closer. He had no children and was very faithful to his pastor and church. He would go to his church every day and fix things. He was there handyman and was very devoted to the house of God. I was impressed by that. I wasn't attending my church regularly at all. I remember the security guard at Comerica stating that Christian's healing was going to come through me. I didn't understand what he meant. He assured me that God was going to heal Chris, but it was going to be according to my faith! I was forever leaving my job to meet Chris at the hospital. Grandma would have to call the EMS and they would send an ambulance. He was having seizures and still not diagnosed. I called early intervention. They evaluated him and ruled out Autism. I had an electroencephalogram (EEG) which detects electrical activity in your brain. He also had an MRI and other tests performed as well.

It was very frustrating not having a diagnosis. So I found comfort in not being alone. To have someone who finally cared. Gino wasn't interested in anything pertaining to Christian. I believe he was ashamed of him. It was hard for him to accept and acknowledge anything coming from him not being perfect. Gino's family wasn't present in his life either. I wrote his mom a letter apologizing for my behavior when I was married to him. I realized that I could have handled the situation differently. I informed her that I was disappointed that she hadn't been active in her grandson's life. I also expressed how disappointed I was to hear that she was so accepting of Gino's mistress. I just assumed because she was a woman of faith that she would encourage her son to reconcile with his family. She responded and informed me that her presence would be limited in Christian's life, if she had to deal with me. So not only was my son rejected by his father, but also his entire family.

Christian was perfect in my eyes. He was my miracle, so it didn't matter if they rejected him. He had plenty of people who absolutely adored him. It was their loss, but it still hurt. I was open to receiving love from Dion and I was open for a real relationship. I didn't know much about him, but what I did know, I liked. He was the youngest of many children. His father had passed away when he was young. He went through some things as a child because of his speech impediment and he was really easy to get along with. The only thing I found strange was that he was a bit secretive. He didn't talk much about past relationships or his personal life. He lived with a friend of his. I assumed the roommate was a male. I was mistaken. Now! This confused me because. Remember I worked at the bank. I saw Dion's checks and he made really good money. So why did he need a roommate?

I asked him just that. He explained that he had lived in another apartment and had to move suddenly and his friend offered her place until he could find somewhere. He told me that I could meet her if I wanted to. Yes, I want to definitely meet her. I met her and she seemed really nice. She complimented me and told him that she liked me and that I seemed really nice. She said he talks about you all the time and that she was glad that he met someone. Dion and I left. He expressed that he really needed me to trust him and that he was not Gino and wouldn't hurt me. He then looked down at my shoes. "Girl if you don't take those ugly shoes off." He then picks me up and cradles me in his arms and takes off my shoes and throws them across the parking lot. I'm screaming for him to put me down. Then I just started laughing. I couldn't believe he did that. I was mad, but then I started laughing.

I love the way he made me feel. He made me feel like a woman. I didn't have to try with him. He just liked me for me. He was very masculine and sexy and we had deep conversations about love and family. He was about 5 feet 10 inches and had very broad shoulders and chest. He was not like any other man I had dated. He was different. There were no arguments or strife between us. He was easy going and he seemed to have a good heart. I felt freedom with him. He wasn't into the night life or the club scene, so I was surprised what happened Sweetest day 1999. He showed up at my place with bags and bags of things for me. He had decided to spend his check on me. He purchased me this beautiful crochet knit dress with the split on the side.

He had bought me several dresses, some boots and shoes. He had me try on every dress and model them for him. Finally, he said that one. Wear that one tonight. It was a black and grey long crochet knit dress with a split on the side. It was very sexy and I felt sexy wearing it. We left and went to a reggae club. I had never been there before. I couldn't believe a club that I hadn't been before. I was surprised. He ordered me a strawberry daiquiri and we sat and talked for a while. I had never seen this side of him before, but I loved the balance. He then leads me to a corner on the dance floor. We had a ball. We danced about three songs, but it was hot in there. I'm not sure if they had the heat on or if it was from us but we left.

We went back to his place. His roommate was out with her boyfriend. They had a balcony attached to the apartment. It was fall, but it was still nice outside.

We made love on the balcony. That was exhilarating. This man was so smooth and sensual that this man seems like a dream come true to me. We were so connected. He made me feel like a real woman. There was nothing that was immature about him. I didn't have to teach him anything naturally or spiritually. We both had a conscious and we knew that this was not the will of God for our lives. In our hearts we knew it, but our flesh was weak. I knew in my spirit that we were sabotaging anything good that we could have. I wanted what I wanted and that always got me into trouble. Same pattern, different man.

Dion was feeling convicted as well and we often discussed it. We were discreet. At this point of our relationship, I was battling so many emotions. I knew that this man was different. There were no signs of other women. I didn't wonder or worry about his whereabouts or who he was with. He was at his church faithfully every Sunday and he seemed almost perfect for me. I thought God had sent me my husband. One Sunday I surprised him and Christian and I showed up at his church. It was a nice small church. He was in the front sitting near the Pastor. He noticed us right away and smiled. After service, he introduced me to a couple of people and asked if we were hungry. He bought us a church dinner and he walked us to my car. I knew that things had shifted between us. When a woman lies with a man she gives of herself. So yet again, all my emotions, my spirit, and my body were given to this man who was not my husband. There was a pull in me for him, because our souls were connected. I thought about him all the time. I imagined him, my son and me as a family. He was a good man with a good heart, yet troubled. He had a lust spirit on him too. That's why we were so drawn to one another. We both needed deliverance from sexual sin, but the door was opened and we had gone too far.

I felt my heart was in the right place when it came to him. My Great Aunt Gwen (Grandma's sister) passed away and my family was devastated. She had been sick for a while with diabetes. Dion went to the services with me and I appreciated that. That night I needed to be alone though. I needed time to grieve. I listened to Fred Hammond's Blessings and Honor all night and I cried. My aunt Gwen was very special to me. Always loving and so giving. I now have another angel. Rest in peace Aunt Gwen. Dion gave me the space I needed and I respected that. I suggested that we get together with my family and their spouses because they were all going to see the new movie The Best Man that was coming out Friday. He agreed so we made plans to meet them at the theater. I was excited for everyone to meet him. I'm not sure if that made him nervous because he was late picking me up.

I called and he wouldn't answer. I called again and he still didn't pick up. I was getting really worried. So I called again. Hours had passed. Dion stood me up, I was embarrassed, I was hurt, and I was angry. Finally, about 11:00 p.m. there is a knock at my door. I'm furious at this point. It's Dion. He comes in the door with an attitude. Saying how he was in Canada with his brothers at a function with his family and how many times I blew up his phone.

"Woman is you crazy?" You called me over 10 times. I politely asked him why didn't he call me back or answer me. He replied that he didn't have a signal. I know a lie when I hear one. I had plenty of practice with Gino. He proceeds to say... "Ummm, Hey, this isn't working, I think that we just need to be friends. I looked at him. "What did you say to me?" He repeated "I think we should take a break and concentrate on being friends." I was starting to boil.

Dion had never seen that side of me. I thought that person was buried when he came into my life, but she was still there. I was trying to hold it in. "Okay Dion, that's fine. Let's be friends." Okay can you please leave now? Dion doesn't leave. Dion can you please leave now? Look, I'm trying to tell this brother to leave because at this point, I'm heated, but I don't want to give him the satisfaction of seeing me boiling. So again, I repeated. "Dion, please leave!" Then he has the nerve to want to explain to me again how I'm acting crazy, I'm possessive. "Whew, girl, I'm asking the Lord is you a stalker?" This man is now berating me. Calling me a stalker, calling me crazy and still didn't leave, after I have asked him over a dozen times to leave. I couldn't hold it any longer. Miki was unleashed.

Dion "GET THE F@#& Out!!!! You are just like the rest of them. Get Out!!!!On that note it was over! I gave Dion exactly what he wanted. Why? Because I knew the signs. I knew something was wrong. Dion wasn't in Canada. Although, he did have family there and often talked about moving to Windsor. "Why on the night you had a date with me, would you go to

Windsor?" It just didn't make any sense. The next day he called me and wanted to talk. He apologized for the way he handled the situation, but still just wanted to be friends. He told me that he really cared about me and cared about Christian and that he still wanted to hang out with us. I apologized for losing my cool and cussing him out.

That following week was really weird for me. Dion still called me. Sometimes I would talk, sometimes I would not. It was difficult for me to transition, to being his friend, after everything we had shared. I was really hurt, but he didn't know. My pride was too important and I refused to give another man that type of power over me. These relationships were making me hard. They were creating a callous over my heart. It was my fault though. When you know better you're supposed to do better. Halloween was approaching and Dion had volunteered for Angel's Night. He informed me that he served with his congregation every year. So I knew I wasn't going to see him that weekend because Angel's night was on a Friday.

The following week, he called and we talked, but he seemed extremely distant. He talked about his church and how they went bowling to fellowship with each other. I thought it was strange that he hadn't mentioned his plans to attend. I just shrugged it off and continued with our conversation. The relationship had definitely shifted. I didn't talk much. I mainly listened to him. He stated that he may be moving to Canada. He said that he would commute daily to his job and that he was excited. I thought that was the most foolish thing I had ever heard, but I just listened. Slowly our conversations became more and more far and in between. I was yearning for him I loved him so much. I would call, but couldn't reach him. It was all very disturbing. He would call sometimes from the phone from his church and leave messages, but that was it. Winter was approaching and there were the usual family gatherings and shenanigans. Gino was sniffing around again.

I was really tired of this merry go round with him. So, I did not oblige. By the beginning of the year I had requested a leave of absence from the bank. Christian was beginning to have more and more seizures. I was calling in more frequently. I realized that my son needed me more than this job. I had to make a sacrifice. I needed to find out why he was having so many seizures and why he still wasn't talking. One night I went to Belle Isle. Christian and I would drive out there often. I would go and talk to God. It started after Gino and I split up sometimes we would sit out there for hours by the water. I felt closer to the Lord near the water. It was always peaceful and serene. I went out there one particular night and asked God to help me with Dion. I knew something wasn't right. I needed answers and I wasn't getting anything from Dion.

At this point I didn't want to push or pry. I didn't want to appear to be this pathetic woman who could not let go! I asked God to help me get over him, to deliver me. I had another soul tie and it was deep. It was January and Dion's birthday was coming up. I didn't have an address for him in Windsor, so I sent a card to his mother's address. I knew her address because we rode by there one day and I saw the house. I never met his mom though. About a week later it was my last day at work. I'm at the window and a young lady comes up. She asked if we could cash her check. She claimed that her bank had been robbed down the street and she didn't have an account. I told her that as long as the check was drawn on Comerica that she could cash it. I asked for her identification. I looked at the address on the I.D. It was Dion's mother's address. I asked her if she knew him. She said, "That's my brother?" "Are you a friend of Dion? I said yes. I asked her how he was doing she said. Oh, he just got married. My face must have fallen to the ground because she immediately tells me how sorry she was.

"Oh my God" He's married??? How long? She stated that it had been a few months. She said that it was rather quickly and that the family barely knew her. I was in total shock. I tried to keep my composure because I was at work, but she could see the tears in my eyes. "I'm sorry. I'm so sorry. Dion has always done things like this. He's a lady's man that's for sure." I was devastated. I gave her the money and thanked her for the information. Now that was divine. God didn't want me to continue to pine over someone who was married to someone else. I went home and cried.

A couple of days later Dion called to thank me for the card. "Congratulations on your marriage." I then hung up the phone. Dion called back. I hung up again. Thirty minutes later he was at my door. I was a mess. I just didn't understand how he could lie to me. I thought he was different. I thought he loved me. I thought that he was a good man because he was in the church and talked about God all the time. I take responsibility for my errors. I should not have slept with him. I made it easy for him. I was too available and desperate. He admitted that he met her at the church's bowling event and that she was related to someone from his church and was invited. He disclosed that he started seeing her while still talking to me. He shared that she was a Principal at a school and that she owned her home. She had him over often doing handy work in her home. They had a rapport with one another. She was looking for marriage also. She had a Master's degree and was very polished. I told him to leave. I just needed the closure. I shouldn't have even opened the door. I just needed to know what happened. Dion left.

He called that evening saying that he knew that he had made a mistake the minute that he got married. It wasn't long before Dion was telling me that he was getting a divorce and leaving his wife. I knew that I shouldn't trust anything that he said. He was proven to be a liar already. It was not long before Dion was calling me and complaining about his marriage. He told me that he should have married me and had made a horrible mistake. He told me that I scared him the night that I called him repeatedly and that made him back off. Between Gino calling and popping over and Dion calling with his apologies and new-found revelations, I was caught up in a whirlwind. I couldn't handle the pressure.

Gino's oldest child's mother connected with me and informed me that she met the young lady with the other two children. She confirmed that they were indeed his sons and suggested that I meet her. I did meet her and the children and she was very sweet and was deceived and lied too as well. It was just too much to process. Christian had three older brothers. Their father didn't claim two of the brothers and here he is rejecting my baby too. Yet, he was still ringing my phone. Why didn't these men just leave me alone? They had obviously chosen who they wanted to be with. Dion had dragged Gino's name so badly into the gutter and called him an idiot for walking out on his marriage and here Dion was walking out on his marriage, trying to have a relationship with me.

So, I left my apartment and moved back with my Grandma. I knew where to go! She was a shield and a protector from all the mess and confusion. Many of my friends thought that I was crazy for moving back to her house. I knew what I was doing. She kept the wolves away. I disappeared. I didn't tell either one of them that I was moving. I was like Casper, I was a Ghost! Well, about 3 months passed and I was fine. Christian and I were at Grandma's it was crowded, but I was okay. Until… one night there was a knock at the door. My Grandmother answered the door. All I could hear was her saying what?? Who?? What do you want? Who? Finally, she yelled for my cousin because she couldn't understand what the person was saying. Then he yelled. "Miki I think this guy is here for you." It was Dion! Remember, he had a speech impediment and sometimes he would stutter if he was nervous. Well I'm sure when my Grandmother opened that door, He was real nervous. She confesses to me later that she knew who he was. She was just being facetious. She told me later that he was so nervous that a big vein popped in the middle of his forehead.

I came out on the porch and Dion tells me how much he loved me and that he was getting a divorce. He just needed me to be patient and give him a little time. He didn't wait for my response he just left. I was torn, ashamed and felt horribly for still being in love with a man who was not my husband. I had become Sylvia. The secret phone calls and meetings for lunch, I was in an affair. I believed every word that Dion spoke to me. I heard the sob stories over and over again, about it not being the right time to leave. He had a step daughter who loved him and looked up to him. He had to plan it and it had to be the right time. Dion pleaded that I was the woman he wanted. I'm so ashamed that I listen to his lies. I'm so ashamed that I believed him.

I had become so low in spirit. I actually justified my wrongdoing. I would speak pure foolishness. "Well he did meet me first." He was never supposed to marry her anyway. He was sent to me and my son. The devil had me believing that I was right in that situation. The devil is a deceiver and a liar. I allowed Satan to manipulate me with thinking that I could actually have a life with someone else's husband. Marriage is honorable and I had always honored it. I was hurt when it happened to me and here I was now in this relationship. There was no justification for my actions. I had reached the bottom of the pit. Dion continued to promise to leave his wife. Over and over again. "In the next two weeks, I'm gone." It was always, "In the next two weeks I'm gone. I was a fool in love and believed his promises. Every promise ended in disappointment.

One night I had a dream. In the dream Dion was in his house with his wife and their little girl. In the dream, they were unaware of my presence, but I could see them. They were lying across the bed in their bedroom watching television. They were laughing, joking and playing. They were a family. It was if God had given me this dream to reveal to me that Dion was lying to me. He wasn't miserable in the dream. They weren't arguing or fighting in the dream. They were happy, they were a family. After the dream, I distanced myself from him and we hadn't spoken in a couple of weeks.

One night, he called and asked to speak with me. I agreed because we needed to have a conversation. He picked me up and we went to a nearby park near the house. I knew there was something heavy on his mind. I proceeded to tell him that what was on my mind and how I could no longer live this way. He then blurted out that he had made a mistake and got his wife pregnant. My mouth dropped, and then I just started thanking God in the car. I started crying and thanking Jesus. I knew that was the one thing that would make me leave him alone. I said. "How do you make a mistake and get your wife pregnant?" I just started laughing hysterically. Then I started thanking God again.

Dion asked me if I would be his mistress. That was the straw that broke the camel's back. How dare he? Well I guess I shouldn't have been surprised. He didn't respect me or his marriage. I had to get out of his truck because I was about to seriously hurt him.

So, I politely got out and started walking home. He begged me to get back in the truck. He had tears in his eyes. I honestly don't think Dion wanted to deliberately hurt me or even his wife for that matter. I just believe Dion was extremely selfish and sick. He had a sickness and a lust spirit and that spirit can and will destroy your life, your body and even your soul. It was over. I had to repent to the Lord for my part in the situation. Dion wouldn't have been able to deceive me, if something wasn't also wrong with me. There was an opening there for him to get in. I had very low self-esteem. I didn't love myself enough to know that this man was full of lies and false promises. I repented to the Lord for participating in this sin. I was broken yet again.

9.

Bewitched

Leading with my heart once again. Seeing all the signs and playing dumb! Naive to see what was right in front of me. Betrayal and deceit, all—over—again. Why, oh why, must I continue to repeat the same mistakes? One night my friend Carol and I decided to hit the bar I was bored and just wanted to get out and dance. There were a couple of attractive guys who came in. They all sat at the bar and one in particular just kept staring at me. I was not impressed because he was not the best looking of the bunch. I thought to myself why is this guy staring so damn hard. UGHHH. I just started to ignore him.

It was fall and the weather was beginning to get cool at night. I was starting a new job at Wayne State University and I wanted to change my image a bit. I paid the money back from when I attended in the early 90's and was taking classes again. I didn't have on a dress or anything sexy this night. I came dressed in a pair of grey slacks and a nice white blouse. My hair was in a curly weave, a look that was cute, but nothing fancy. Carol and I were on the dance floor at Chucks Millionaires Club. That had become our spot. We loved to hang out there on Mondays and Thursdays. We would hustle, ballroom and sometimes just get on the floor and dance in the mirrors. We would always have a ball and we were regulars at the bar. They had the best strawberry daiquiris.

I was no longer going to church. I felt that if I attended church and hung at the club, I would be considered a hypocrite, so I stopped attending church. I wasn't ready to give up dancing at the clubs. I loved the atmosphere. I didn't want to live a double life so I left the church. I know, I know. I was really confused. I had been divorced about three years and had gone through a lot with Gino and then Dion. I was back living at home with my Grandmother. There was so much drama going on at the house. My brothers and cousins were fighting all the time and life was a bit depressing. I was so ready to move again.

My Grandmother knew that I was going through some things and she offered to watch Chris so that I could get out and have some fun. She knew that I was still hurting from the divorce and this was a way for me to release stress. I was a single parent and times were a bit difficult. This was her way of giving me a little relief. I would wait for him to get to sleep and leave out for a little adult fun. Well anyway the guy continues to stare at me. Finally, I got up and started to hustle because my jam had come on. He continued to watch me and I was thinking, Oh No buddy, it is not going to happen. After the hustle segment ended, a slow jam came on and I saw him rise from the chair and head towards me. UT oh, here he comes. He grabs my hand, but wait! It was the way he grabbed it that got my attention. He almost commanded my attention. He asked me to dance with him.

As you already know, I absolutely love to dance, so I obliged him. As he walked me to the dance floor, I really got a good look at him. He was about 5 feet 8 slightly overweight, pimples and… Not my type at all!!! Despite his looks, he was really a good ballroom dancer. As we danced he whispered different instructions in my ear. When to turn, when to double spin and so forth. It was if he was entertaining everyone or putting on a show instead of just dancing with me. Although, I was confused about his display, I liked it. Because that's what I would do when I went out. It was a way of escape, a way for me to release everything. I absolutely loved to ballroom dance, it's so therapeutic.

He could dance; he was smooth, not easy on the eyes at all, but very confident. He asked if I knew how to salsa. I told him no. He offered to teach me if I wanted to learn. I declined. After the dance, he politely thanked me and that was it. I could feel him watching, but I ignored him. Shortly after we left. This guy had enticed me with one dance. It wasn't what he did. It was how he did it. I could feel the strength of his arms and the intensity in his eyes, as he looked at me to follow his lead. He was intensely alluring despite his looks. There was a sexiness about him. As we were leaving the bar, he was outside sitting in his car. "Where are you ladies going?" Y' all are not about to walk out here alone. Wait a minute. Oh no we are fine! We're good. He gets out the car and walks with us untill we are safely to the car. He then hands me his business card and introduced himself. "Hi, I'm Leonard and you are?" He told me that he was into marketing and that he had just moved back to Detroit from Vegas. He seemed really business-oriented and important. I was impressed. He wasn't the most handsome guy in the club, but he was a gentleman and I liked that.

I went home. I called Leonard about a week later he didn't answer so I left a message. He returned my call about a day later. He said that he was in California with a few of his friends. He asked if he could take me out when he got back. I told him to just give me a call. Leonard called and we went to the movies. This guy bragged a lot. He told me that he had 2 children. Okay, that's cool. That he had been in Vegas for about 10 years that he had made all this money, had a Benz and an Infinity that he bought for his wife. He *was* married, but now recently divorced. It was too much information. I just wanted a movie and some popcorn.

The courtship was very slow. I really wasn't feeling Leonard at all, but he had charisma. He was a charmer and he made me laugh a lot. I thought well this won't be a love connection, but I could see myself hanging out with him. He's funny and entertaining and a great ballroom dancer. Once upon a time though you could see that he was a very handsome man. A few weeks passed and Leonard and I were hanging like wet clothes. He was actually a really cool person. He would call me up and say

Hey let's go to a movie, or let's go to dinner. I have tickets for a concert, or simply let me cook dinner for you. He was very assertive, spontaneous and I loved that. He was starting to wear me down. He lived in Auburn Hills in a beautiful condo. He would invite me over and just chill and talk. He was interested in what I had to say and how I felt about things. He loved the fact that I was in school and educated. He always had the ambiance in his place just right. Music playing and just the right lighting.

Leonard was a hopeless romantic and I liked that about him. About 3 months had passed and things were beginning to progress. We both wanted to take our time and really get to know each other. Then one night it happened. I came over and he had white candles lit in the living room and in the bedroom. The stereo was blasting with Luther. He loved Luther. Hey! I was ready. It had been a long time, I wasn't waiting on a husband and I wasn't waiting on Love. I had given up on those things. I was just a grown woman in her 30's, who knew what she wanted. It wasn't even about him it was about me and my wants. I wasn't looking for a relationship. I wasn't looking for love. I just wanted to have sex and we did.

Afterwards we took a shower and I started to get dressed and preparing myself to leave. He was a bit confused. "Where are you going?" I'm leaving! Why are you leaving? He seemed really surprised. I just wasn't going to set myself up anymore. I knew what this was. We enjoyed each other's company and that was that. No more heartbreak for me. Those days were over. Leonard told me that he didn't want me to leave and asked was I hungry. We ate and then he asked if we could possibly get out of town and maybe take a weekend trip together. Uh I guess. I was thinking what is this guy up too? Is he playing a game with me? A trip? What the hell is he talking about? Yeah okay, yeah, we will see. Leonard was persistent he knew that I wasn't really trying to be with him. Maybe that was a challenge for him because he laid it on strong.

He called a lot and always had some plans. I really liked that because it was refreshing to date a man who was on a mission. Leonard moved to Livonia which was much closer to me, so we saw one another often. I worked as a student assistant at Wayne State. I loved the job because it was in an office and I was able to work in between my classes. It was very convenient. I really didn't talk to Gino anymore. He wasn't seeing my son or helping out at all. He had officially become a deadbeat dad. Gino had spread a horrible rumor that Christian wasn't his son. I was told this information by someone close to the family. Well that was his way of not taking responsibility, by denying he was the father. He had done it twice before and now with our child. No paternity test, no nothing. Although, he was my husband and our son was conceived in love. He denied him. The cycle repeats and I was distraught; he was saying and doing anything to tarnish my name.

Christian was in school and was attending Poe Developmental School. He had been attending the school since he was 3 years old. He first attended Early on and took classes at the Day School of the Deaf Center. I absolutely loved that school. It was close to Wayne State so I would drop him off, run to class and then on to work. My life was full and I loved it. I was focused, for the first time, in a long time. I felt like my life had purpose again. Christian was learning and had a great teacher at Poe. The principal was phenomenal and the staff really cared about the students. Leonard hadn't met my son. After my experience with Dion, I promised myself I would not expose my son to anyone else unless I knew they were serious.

The holidays were approaching and Leonard came by and dropped off a Christmas gift for me and Christian. I hadn't bought him anything and felt bad. I thought that the gesture was thoughtful and gracious. As time progressed I spent more time with Leonard. He would invite me over for dinner and he cooked a lot. Baked chicken, grilled fish and sautéed vegetables were his specialty. He was the best host, I would come by and he would always hand me a glass of wine and have the music playing on the stereo. One night my phone kept ringing. I admit I was still hanging out and having fun. I was still single; we hadn't decided to be exclusive. Sometimes, I would exchange numbers with someone, but it was all in fun.

So anyway, when my phone rang, it really wasn't a big deal that I didn't answer. Leonard looked disturbed. The phone rang again so I answered. There was a guy on the other end. I don't even remember meeting him. We spoke for a moment and I informed him that I was in the middle of something and hung up. Leonard's whole disposition shifted. He was angry and he told me that I needed to leave and accused me of trying to play him. I tried to explain that I didn't even remember the guy. That made it worse, so I left. I called him when I got home and he didn't answer. I left him several messages. I should have just left it alone. Leonard had abandonment issues just like me. His wife had left him. She was much younger and very attractive. Apparently, she left him like a thief in the night. He didn't know where she was. I believe that he was guarded because of that situation and felt I was playing a game with him. We didn't talk for a few days. When he did return my call, it was as if nothing had occurred.

My argument was why was he so upset? I didn't understand because he had many female friends. He knew a lot of people. We started to argue with each other. That was the first time that I noticed his mouth. He was very insensitive and started to curse at me. Well, I was familiar with this kind of situation and I wasn't about to let him talk to me any kind of way so I went off on him. I then hung up the phone and went to Yesterdays. I walked into Yesterdays and guess who is there? Standing and watching me. I didn't let his presence intimidate me at all. I was in my comfortable space and I was cooler than a fan. I danced, ballroom and totally ignored him. It wasn't long before he was grabbing me by my hand and leading me to the dance floor. He knew how much I loved to ballroom. The Deejay plays Kem "Love Calls."

We danced. It was very sensuous and slow. He could dance that's for sure. He had since left his marketing job and was working for SBC. We didn't really talk about the incident and just picked up where we had left off. As time passed we had become a couple. I met his mom and his family. I absolutely adored his mother, she was so cool and sweet. She went to church and loved the Lord. She really liked me and would always tell him that I was sweet and a good woman. Leonard was street, he knew how to turn it on and turn it off. He was a professional when it pertained to business, but he was hood too. I liked that about him, it kind of turned me on. He knew how to hustle and make things happen for himself. He didn't wait for anyone to give anything to him. Some would say that he was an opportunist, but what did he want with me? I didn't have anything and sometimes he would say it.

Slowly he had began to belittle me and chip away at my self-esteem. Little comments here and there. They were subtle, but I was aware. Comments about my clothes, my weaves or my shoes. More and more little by little. He would say I didn't have any class and that I was broke as a joke. He always made comments about my lack of finances. His comments were becoming increasingly insulting and demeaning. He would say things like, "I'm the best man that you have ever had and I lived in Vegas and I had a 2200 square foot home." Everything had begun to shift. Our relationship had turned into a War of Words. That's what we did. When we were good, we were good, but when we were bad it was horrible. I don't know why I didn't leave him. I should have run for the hills. Such disrespect, I didn't value myself or love myself enough to leave him. I just retaliated with words to attack and insult him.

I would talk about his fat belly and gut and his receding hairline. In one argument, I even called him "Homer" He was confused. "Who the hell is Homer?" he asked. I said. "Duh!" Homer Simpson and then I hung up the phone. Every time he called back I would say. "Duh!" and hang up. I was desensitized and believed that this was normal behavior. Leonard wore suits because of his job. He presented himself like he was Mr. GQ himself. My friends were appalled and couldn't believe that I was dating this guy. They all thought that he was ugly inside and out. My cousins had nicknamed him Jerome from Martin. I also later found out that he had five children, not two. He had an older son and daughter in their twenties. They had different mothers and a son who was 5 years old in Vegas who resided with his mother. As well as, the two children with the same Mom that lives here.

He was reluctant to disclose that information, but eventually confessed it to me. Everyone was very confused because they were accustomed to me dating very attractive men and he was the total opposite of anyone I had dated. One night I had stayed the night and I had always noticed candles burning in his living room, but these particular candles were covered in aluminum foil. I thought it was strange and asked him about it. He shrugged it off and said that he was preserving the candles. For what?! Something just didn't sit right with me about it, so when Leonard was asleep, I went in the living room and began to remove the foil. I couldn't believe my eyes, there were hearts all over the candles. With arrows and pictures of cupid with the bow and arrow.

Words such as, Come to me!!! Marry me!!! Love Me, were written all over the red candles. There were two of them burning constantly. "Oh my God this man is into voodoo." I got the hell out of there. No wonder, I dealt with his foolishness and his verbal abuse.

Leonard called me the next day and wanted to know why I left. I told him that we needed to talk. We met the next day at Fridays. I confronted him about the candles and he denied that it was witchcraft. He laughed at me and said that he just loves candles and that candles set the mood. I agreed with him. I like candles too, but I don't burn candles with hearts with arrows and cupid on them. Leonard tried to justify his activities and even told me that they burn candles in the bible.

He even told me that he uses oils when meeting clients to make people like him. He justified it with the use of incense, myrrh and oils in the Bible. I informed Leonard that he was playing with fire and that he was dabbling in divination. I explained that he was manipulating situations with the oils and candles. He told me that he received the candles from his aunt, who was also a preacher. "I DON'T CARE WHERE YOU GOT IT FROM." Y'all are practicing witchcraft and divination.

Leonard expressed that he wasn't aware that it was a sin. He promised to stop burning the candles if they offended me. I tried to explain to him that it just wasn't good and that he was opening the door to the devil and demonic influence and attacks. I'm sure he didn't take me serious considering I was in sin with him. How could I educate him about spiritual things and we were sharing a bed? He didn't take me serious. He thought I was a hypocrite and a joke. Needless to say, the candles were gone. I continued to see Leonard even though I saw all the signs that he was not the one. I was lonely and he was there. He told me that he and his brother had to go to a training. He was going to be gone the weekend of my birthday.

That was a bummer and I was so upset about it. I had planned a party at Yesterday's night club and was so excited. Leonard told me that he would make it up to me but he had to go to California for training with his job. He explained that it was mandatory. So, I just dealt with it and proceeded with my birthday party plans. Anyway, I drive him to the airport and its kissy face and baby I will be back soon. My birthday comes and goes and I make the best of it although I missed his presence. It all sounded very suspicious, but I was giving him the benefit of the doubt. He called me every night, but didn't stay on the phone long.

One day I talked to him and I asked what he was doing and he replied that he was walking on the beach. The conversations were long enough to ask me about my day, brief me on his and then off to bed because he was tired. Finally, he arrives home after being gone for about 4 days. Christian and I are at his apartment while he's at work. I would be there answering the phone, relaxing, whatever. This particular day, Christian is in his room on his dresser and grabs a piece of paper off of his dresser. "Chris what is this you have baby?" I looked at the paper it is a receipt. Guess what? The receipt is from a restaurant in Hawaii. I look at the date and it is the same date when Leonard was supposed to be in California. So immediately I was furious! I called my male friend Sammy. He tells me to get out of there. Now!!! He reminds me that I have my son and that I didn't need to get in any altercation or confrontation while he was present. He talked some sense in to me that day. So, I decided to leave Leonard with a little note. I looked in my make-up bag and found the reddest lipstick that I could find and wrote CALIFORNIA HUH??? In bright red letters across his bathroom mirror and attached the receipt to the mirror. I avoided his calls for a week.

As usual, he had an explanation. He admitted that the trip was pre-planned way before he met me and that he always traveled with his friends. He didn't know how to tell me without it being a tumultuous situation so he lied. The lies were getting bigger and bigger. He started working for a new company and started meeting a lot of new people and clients. Leonard started hosting these parties at the Comfort Zone, promoting Thursday night, after work affairs. The name of the party was Hypnotic Nights after the name of a new liquor that came out. Leonard hosted parties to promote the liquor and the club.

I never attended his parties, but I did assist him with promoting them. We would go out and pass out flyers and leave them on people's car. I did that to support his vision although I was totally against it. I was not thrilled about it and I just felt like we were too old to be in the clubs. We both were getting older and I didn't feel that was an atmosphere that we should be a part of all the time. Although we met in the club, I believe it was time to leave and settle down. I was growing and evolving and I didn't want that life anymore. I was getting tired, so I would not go out with him. He went out more and more though. I did it for him. One night I was going to stop by and ended up just cruising.

Back when Gino and I first separated, I would do a drive by his house. I hadn't done that in years, but this particular night I did. So I'm riding down the street and lo and behold, he whips out the drive way behind me. Oh My God!! I am caught! He flashes his lights and pulls me over, like he was the police or something. I slowly roll down my window. He says, "Sooo, how long have you been doing this?" I couldn't do anything but laugh. I responded. "Well actually it's been years". There was nothing I could say. He asked where I was headed? I told him that I was debating meeting my boyfriend out at the club. I explained that he hosted at the club and how I really wasn't feeling that atmosphere. He asked if I wanted to take a drive. I said, sure.

We rode around cruising like we did back in the day. We resolved a lot from the past and I talked to him mainly about having a relationship with his son. I also confronted him about the horrid rumor that he was spreading about Chris. Of course, he denied it. He came up with some lie about a woman told his mother that. The same cycle repeating. I told him that I was back in school and would need his assistance with making sure that Chris gets inside the school on Tuesdays and Thursdays. I had a biology class and I was late every session because of the scheduling. I asked him for this one thing and he said that he would do that for me. We talked for hours, finally we looked up and it was 1:00 in the morning. Leonard was blowing my phone up! Is that your dude Gino asked? Yes, I replied. I better answer it. I answered the phone and Leonard wanted to see me. Gino returned me back to my car. Needless to say, he never assisted me with Christian's school situation. It was years before I saw him again.

So anyway, the following week on a Thursday, I decided to pop up at Hypnotic Nights. Yes, I did. I popped up. You know sometimes you have to do that just to check things out and keep people on their toes. Just to see what's really going on. I walked in and immediately his brother saw me. "Heyyyy Sis, what you doing here? His eyes were big as saucers when he saw me. Like Whoa… She's here Big! "Hey Bro, I wanted to check out Hypnotic Nights. I see y'all have a nice crowd." He didn't know what to do or what to say. He just leads me to the bar. "What are you drinking sis, I got you!" Chardonnay. He orders my glass of wine.

I look around the room looking for Leonard. He is nowhere in sight. I look more thoroughly and there he is on the dance floor with this chick. She had on a short mini dress, but she looked tore up from the floor up. I knew immediately that they were familiar with each other by the way that she danced with him. I sat there, held my cool and observed. I watched. I watched intensely. I watched the way she moved. I watched how he responded. All while Leonard's little brother thought that he had me entertained with his conversation. After the dance, Leonard came over. "Hey baby what are you doing here?" Oh, I came out to experience Hypnotic Nights. You talk so much about it and how every Thursday the crowd is growing. I came to check it out and to be supportive. "Oh, I can't be here?" Of course you can baby, I just thought I would see you later at the house. You know this is where I do my networking and I don't want you getting jealous if you see me talking to women or what not. This is business baby. That's all. I looked at him. "Who is that girl you were dancing with?" I asked. "Here you go, here you go! I'm out here networking! I'm trying to make some money. I'm trying to make a name for myself. Here you come with this drama. Oh, never drama I just asked a simple question. That's my friend she is somebody that is supporting me and who I network with. No big deal. Why are you tripping on her? Hmmm. I continued to sip on my wine.

I notice that the young lady is watching Leonard and me. That gave me even more indication that something was not right. So, I leave it alone. He walks away, "Baby let me know if you need anything." If you're hungry or anything, but I have to work the room. I said hmmm. Okay go ahead and network. While he is walking around the room and conversing with individuals, she continues to watch me. She and a Caucasian woman, who I assume was her friend, then get up and go into the bathroom. So I get up from the bar and go to the bedroom. I walk in and the young lady is in the stall, but her friend is in the mirror. I began to touch up my makeup. "Girl this club is jumping tonight! I'm so happy that my man has a crowd. We have been passing out flyers all week." The friend looked confused. "Who is your man?" she asked. "Leonard" Leonard is my man!" She expressed a look of shock and horror. "Tonya, isn't Leonard your man?" There was a voice coming from the stall that was low and timid. "No" Her friend was irritated. "Girl didn't you help him pass out flyers for this event today?" She still didn't respond.

I begin to question her. "Are you sure there isn't anything going on between you and Leonard?" Girl you know these men can be players and I really need for you to tell me the truth if anything is going on between you two." "No, we are just friends." I looked at her for a long time, Okay!!! Her friend asks, "Where are you sitting?" I informed them that I was at the bar. Tonya's friend invited me to sit with them. As we walked out the bathroom, I could see Leonard's eyes gazing toward the door. He looked as if he was about to poop in his pants. I walked confidently to their table and sat with them.

Leonard tried to play it cool, but he was worried. Tonya's friend started to probe me with all kinds of questions and I answered every one of them. Tonya was silent. It wasn't too long before Leonard was motioning for me to come over to him. I politely walked over to hear what he had to say. "What are you doing sitting with them? Oh aren't they your friends? What's the problem? I don't want you sitting with them. Why not? Because her friend is gay and she may try to slip something in your drink or something. I could see right through the bull. That woman is not gay Leonard. You are tripping! I'm good boo. Finish your networking. I'm about to go back to the table. "If you don't go sit your ass back at the bar." I double back, Excuse me? I started to laugh, because I knew then that Leonard was caught. So I went back to the table and observed. I knew that it was only a matter of time before Tonya would confront Leonard.

Low and behold she was face to face with him. She whispered in his ear. There was an exchange of words and then she walked away. He was pissed. I knew then that it was time to go. I got the information that I needed. As I headed toward the door. Leonard grabs me and asks to meet at his place. I informed him that it was not going to happen. "I'm going home Leonard". What's wrong with you? Let me go Leonard, I'm going home. I walk out the club. As I'm walking getting ready to go to my car, I hear a voice.

Hey excuse me, are you leaving? It was Tonya. Yes, I'm leaving. Awww well, it was nice meeting you! Yep! You too. Long pause. Wait! I lied to you earlier. Leonard and I were seeing each other. I know all about you. We have been in bed and you have called. He would tell me to be quiet while he talked to you. Most times he would rush you off the phone. I know all about your little boy. You have a son right? I have seen your things at the house. Such as clothes and make up. He told me you were this horrible person and when I met you tonight. I knew that everything that he said about you was a lie. Tears begin to stream down my face. As the tears roll, it starts to rain. Leonard comes outside.

Get the hell away from here. Why are you lying to her? She deserves to know the truth. Tonya replied. They begin to argue. Leonard's family comes outside to calm him down. Tonya is cursing him out. "This girl is nice" She is a sweet girl, that's why I had to tell her the truth. You are lowdown and dirty Leonard. I slowly walk away. Neither of them is aware that I'm leaving. I get in my car and the next thing I remember is I'm in my Grandma's driveway. I don't even remember the ride home. I was devastated. While I'm trying to process this information, I call Carol and its 2:00 in the morning. She answers. She is in St. Louis on a women's retreat with her family's church. I'm crying and explain to her what happened. She prays for me….

Dion called me, even though we were over. Periodically he would call to check on me. He knew that I was in a relationship and was unhappy in it. I confided in him about Leonard. He asked if he could talk to me in person. I agreed. He came by and apologized to me for everything. He told me that he needed to repent to me for his actions. He also stated that he believed because of his treatment towards me that it affected my self-esteem even more. He said Leonard was a loser and that I deserved so much better than him. He acknowledged that our situation had further damaged me and he was sorry for his contribution in my bad choices. I accepted his apology and forgave him. It was the closure that I needed to close that chapter in my life.

Two weeks passed and I haven't heard a word from Leonard. Not that I was expecting too. There was a lot of drama that night and he was cold busted! I mean seriously what could he say? What explanation could possibly justify his actions? I was cool and realized that all my intuitions were valid.

You know a woman knows when something isn't right. I was relieved to know that I wasn't crazy and my suspicions were authentic. I wasted so much time with him and it was over.

Then, the lights when out. It was August 14, 2003 and the city went black. I was working at a grocery store on Warren. The job was part-time and I wanted to make some extra money for the summer. It was a cashier position and I didn't like working there at all, but hey, it was a job. We were not allowed to even talk at that store. If we showed any type of laughter or joy, he would ask, "Hey what's so funny over there? You ladies need to get back to work." It was definitely something I had never experienced before. All of a sudden everything goes black. The lights suddenly go out, fortunately there was a generator at the store. So we still had to work.

The cash registers were computerized so we had to use paper and pencil to make transactions. People were rushing in buying ice, candles, you name it. We had to stay because it was so busy. On top of that it was scorching hot! Boy was it hot! The temperature had to be about 95 degrees that day. When I finally arrived home, everyone was outside. My brothers and cousins were trying to make accommodations for the house. My grandmother had my son and was also sitting on the porch. Christian was just happy to see me. He began to touch my nose and kiss me on the cheek. All of a sudden, my phone rings. It's Leonard. "Are you and Christian alright?" Yes, we're fine I answered. Well. My apartment has a generator and there is air conditioning here and partial power. I don't want you and Chris in the dark.

You both are welcome to come here. I listen… So you wait until a blackout to get the courage to call me? Courage, why would I need courage? That girl lied to you. She played you and just wanted to get you out of the picture and you fell for it. She did the punk-fake. She admitted that she saw your things there. She knew that you were my woman. She wanted me, so she got rid of you. We did not have sex, she lied.

No, you're lying, that girl wouldn't have gone through the trouble of following me out that club if you two weren't involved. Just tell the truth. Okay! You and Chris come out here so that we can talk. I will tell you everything. I went to Leonard's apartment and we talked, it wasn't long before we were back together.

As the months passed, Leonard and I just existed. I began to question everything. God was giving me all the signs and I was ignoring those signs. One night I was at his apartment and we were coming back from the movies and something told me, "Your tire is flat.". I shunned it off and thought okay I'm tripping. Why would my tire be flat? Sure enough, the next morning when I left, my tire was flattened to the ground. I demanded to know what was going on. Leonard played stupid. Nothing is going on. I told him that he needed to come clean with me. He continues to deny. I insisted that he reveal the cold-hearted ugly truth. Don't worry baby, I'm going to get your tire fixed. Well, I'm going with you because I need to be there. I need to be aware and know if someone is slashing my tire or what?

What is really going on? This is crazy, but for whatever reason I didn't go. I don't even understand why I didn't. Leonard convinced me to stay at his apartment and to allow him to handle it. That's why I believe this man had voodoo on me because I walked 5 blocks to find that Nika girl with Gino, nothing or no one could stop me from doing anything that I wanted to do. So now that I looked back on it. Yes, I believe that I was being manipulated and influenced.

The relationship was not going anywhere and was beginning to deteriorate. I didn't trust him and because of the lack of trust, we argued a great deal. Leonard was the king of profanity. This relationship wasn't like my other relationships where I dominated in the arguments. I had definitely met my match in the battle of words. He was a master at his craft. As spring arrived, things begin to shift. His job was putting a lot of demands on him. Things were not going well, which stressed him out. When a person is stressed they do desperate things. Leonard sat me down one day and told me that he was thinking about going to Atlanta for a job.

What kind of job is it? I asked. Its construction, we are building a new company. He assured me that they paid good money and that once the job was completed, that he would be back. I was puzzled. My instincts told me that Leonard was lying, but I played the game. Never let them see you sweat. That had become my motto. So although I knew that was some BS I didn't say anything. Within weeks, I noticed that Leonard had ended his lease and left his job at the internet company. Again, I questioned him about the job in Atlanta. He assured me that he was on a leave from his permanent job and had previously made arrangements. As the day approaches, I'm getting more and more irritated. I know something isn't quite right about this spontaneous move. The day Leonard leaves, he stops by and reassures me that he will be back before I know it. He kisses me and leaves. He was driving down to Atlanta and later that evening, I receive a frightening phone call.

Leonard's children's mother had died in an accident. I was horrified and tried desperately to reach him. After several attempts he answered, he was absolutely distraught. He was crying and extremely upset. Instantly, my heart went out to him and I tried to console him. He was hurting for his children and their mother. I assumed that he would turn the car around and come back home, but he didn't. He pursued with his destination to Atlanta. He claimed that he was tired and needed to rest. A few days later he returned for the services. There was a whole new dynamic to the equation because Leonard now had two children to raise.

Whenever I called him, sometimes I could reach him and other times I couldn't. One night my phone rang. It was Leonard's phone number, so I answered instantly. I could hear a woman's voice on the other end of the phone. She was telling Leonard that she was hungry and requesting him to make her a sandwich. "Hello, Hello," no response. Then the phone goes dead. I immediately called back and I repeatedly got his voicemail. I left a message. Two days passed before Leonard responded. When he did call, he denied everything. I realize that he was a habitual liar. Later that week I go to the mall and I see his two older children. They tell me everything. Apparently, Leonard and this woman Dana, his so called best friend, has been involved for over 15 years. She has always been in his life and it didn't matter to her who he dated or even married. She just stood by the way side and waited until it was over. She had always been a constant in his life. I stood there and listen to his children tell me their torrid history. They were very apologetic for their father's deception. I went home. I sat in my car for about an hour. My Aunt Bunnie was at the house and knew I was upset. She tried to get me to confide in her. I shared the information that was conveyed to me.

She gave me a pep talk and had turned my tears into laughter. She always made me feel better. Eventually, Dana called me. I was expecting that call She begins to tell me that she has a 2800 square foot home with a three-car garage. That she drives a Benz and has two degrees including a Masters. I listened and demanded to know the purpose of the call. "He's there with you right?" I asked. So why are you calling me?" I don't want him, "Girl you can have that headache. "Hey, have you ever heard of Juanita Bynum?" I suggest that you get her tape. "No More Sheets." "It's about women who are tied to ungodly relationships." The more she spoke, the more I felt sorry for her. She's bragging about her home and her cars yet she's on my line.

She informs me that she was pregnant and loss the baby and Leonard is coming back because he has no money and her bills need to be paid. Clearly, Leonard had used and played this girl for years and she also needed to be free. As a woman, my heart went out to her. I just wanted to know why she would waste 15 years of her life on someone who didn't love her enough to make her his wife. So I asked that very question. She explained that she was married and that she separated from her husband when he decided to come to Atlanta. She revealed that his children were currently living there in her house. She then attempts to prove that he's there and puts him on the intercom to solidify her claim. "Hey honey is dinner ready?" she asked. "Dinner is ready!" he responded. I was amused. I told her that my son and I lived in one room out of my Grandma's house. I congratulated her on all of her accolades that she felt necessary to share with me. I wished them well and hung up the phone.

My Granddaddy Daniel was a very special person to me. We had begun to have a relationship. I would call him and talk to him all the time. He went through a depression when my Grandmother died. Who could blame him, they had been together for 50 years of their lives. He went to the cemetery every day to visit her grave. I tried to explain to him that maybe Grandma Belle would want him to try to go on with his life. And that she was at peace with God. He went faithfully every day until Granddaddy was diagnosed with prostate cancer. He received treatments, but the cancer came back and eventually started to spread. I received a call from my dad that he was in hospice. I was so hurt, why is he in hospice? I visited my Granddaddy and told him that I wanted to take care of him. That he needed to come home with me. He wasn't hearing it though. "Baby I worked for

Chrysler thirty years. I paid to have this. No, you have my grandson to raise. I will not be a burden on you."

I pleaded with my Granddaddy, but he was stubborn and wouldn't change his mind. "Listen, when are you going back to church?" he asked. I stared at him for a second because I was not trying to go there. "Granddaddy, I go to church." I replied. "Girl you are not in church the way you were before, going every blue moon isn't being in church. "I need you to go back and rededicate your life to God." You were so happy when you first got saved. I need you to do this for me. Ok? Promise me that you will. "I will Granddaddy."

He continued, "You need to slow down, you are hanging out and dating these no-good men. "God is going to send you a husband." I interrupted him. "Granddaddy I'm fine. I'm not thinking about a husband." "Girl, who do you think you are talking too?" I know you! You want to be married. God is going to send you a husband who is going to love you and your little boy. Trust me and it's going to be sooner than you think." "I love you Granddaddy." I kissed him on the forehead and left. I didn't want him to see my tears. The next day, I went to Bible study and when they called for the backslider to come home, I went to the altar. The next day I called my Granddaddy on my way to class and shared my news. He was pleased; he sounded weak and said that he was tired. I told him that I would be there tomorrow to see him. My Granddaddy died the next day.

I heard through the grapevine that Leonard was coming back to Detroit. I was determined to not fall back in the same snares as before. I knew that he left me to start a life in Atlanta with Dana. He was a snake, he deceived me, but I still was connected to him. I had so much compassion for his children and wanted to be there for them. My heart especially was connected to his little girl because I knew losing a mother leaves a void. His cousin expressed to me how remorseful he was for his lies and deception. She told me that he realized how much he really cared for me. I didn't know who or what to believe.

I was back in church and trying to live right. I needed no distractions. Leonard did come home and moved into a house on the Westside. Whenever we would see one another, I would have my worship music playing in the car. I wasn't trying to go backwards. I wanted to move forward with my life. We would go to the movies and he even visited church with me.

His hands were up like Ayeee!!! Dancing like he was at the club, it was cool though. I actually thought it was kind of funny. It reminded me when I first came in that move something dress. At least he was coming and trying to get more understanding of the Word. He made remarks suggesting we live together, but that wasn't going to happen. I made a vow after Gino to never shack again. That was so wrong and disrespectful to live in my Grandmother's house with him before we were married. During that time, I didn't know any better, but I do now. My son and I moved out and I absolutely love having my own home and having a sense of freedom. Christian and I were finally stable and content. His dad still wasn't in his life, but I had even accepted that. I was at a place of peace concerning that situation. I saw Gino on Plymouth one day at the traffic light. I looked over, he nodded and I nodded and that was it. Sylvia was in the car, but she wasn't positioned for me to see her face. I have never laid eyes on her. There were times that I would see him driving on the street and would literally chase him down in my car to berate him about his son. I was glad I was finally moving forward. Deliverance feels so good.

I was in school and completing classes for my plan of work. Every semester there was a sense of accomplishment and I was beginning to see the light at the end of the tunnel. I was enjoying my new life. The only thing was living in the house alone. Sometimes it was too quiet and I was uncomfortable. I was accustomed to hearing arguing and fighting breaking out in the middle of the night. This occurred a lot at my Grandma's house and I needed for my son to be in a happier and stable environment. The calmness and the quiet of the night were sometimes uneasy for me, that's crazy. I had to adjust to our new life that God had given us.

Leonard was upset with me. He made a statement about how broke I was and now that I have a home I'm acting different. I knew that I wanted to live a different life. I was changing and Leonard was up to his old tricks again. His daughter who was eleven informed me that he was seeing someone. She said, "My dad is the number one liar." I asked her baby why you would say that. That's when she told me that he was seeing this young lady from his past. I believe it was an old girlfriend and they'd rekindled their relationship. I confronted him about the young lady and once again he denied it. He knew that he was losing me and he did not like it. I wasn't the same insecure woman from before. I was getting stronger and my faith was increasing again.

He comes to my house with a ring in a little plastic bag. "Where is the box?" I asked. "Baby this is your engagement ring, but it's not ready yet I need to get it dipped in platinum first." Hmmm, dipped in platinum? Why does it have to be dipped? Shouldn't it already be platinum? I assured him that we were not ready for marriage. Our relationship was damaged; too much had occurred. Of course, we argued. That was our normal, but it was all becoming a bit redundant. Leonard suggested that we take a break to date other people. I agreed because I knew there was some validity in his daughter's story. I obliged and didn't dispute the break because I was tired of the merry-go-round. I wanted marriage and I also wanted a family and Leonard was adamant about not having more children.

We both wanted different things. Leonard and I no longer shared the same desires and values and it was time to completely let go. We didn't part hating one another and if I ever needed him, he would have moved mountains to make sure I had what I needed. He loved being needed and he loved making things happen. We had just outgrown each other.

Love Nots

10.

No Fairytale, It's Work

I met my husband taking care of business for my Grandma. I'm standing in a line and boy was it long. I saw a handsome, distinguished gentleman at the counter. His demeanor was mean......Oh NO. I hope I don't get him. Just my luck, I'm starring in the face of this man. He spoke and I explained my situation and that I was there on behalf of my Grandmother. He was actually quite helpful. I noticed his hands, they looked soft, well-manicured, as if he had never worked a hard day in his life. On his right hand was a black opal ring. I asked him. "Are you married?" his reply, "No". He asked. "Are you?" NO! I replied. He then slid me a piece of paper to write my name and number. WE exchanged information. "Hey, disregard my outfit. I'm a humdinger under this baseball cap!" I stated. I was dressed in some jogging pants with a sweatshirt and a baseball cap. I didn't even have on make up this day. That was the line that hooked him. He called me that evening and I was quite surprised he called me the same day. That was definitely different. Some men have to be so macho and make the woman wait. Okay, so Mark called me and we talked on the phone that night to about 1 a.m. in the morning. He expressed that he was not a phone person, but enjoyed our conversation so much that he couldn't hang up the phone.

He was working two jobs at the time so his time was limited. Before he met me, he would work, come home, take a nap and then off to his evening job. We decided to go to the movies. Mark was supposed to call me so that we could make plans for a Tuesday. No call. So, finally he calls and I tell him that maybe we shouldn't talk anymore. And that I didn't like men who do not keep their word. He claimed that he had been called into work and had forgotten to call me so that we could make plans. I hung up the phone. Mark, called back immediately asking why did I hang up. He asked me not to ever do that again and to always talk to him. I admit that impressed me. Most men are so full of themselves and their egos would have never called back. He apologized and we made plans to go out.

We were supposed to meet at the movie theater in Birmingham. We were going to see Mr. and Mrs. Smith. So, I'm standing in front of the Palladium, waiting for Mark to show up and there is no Mark in sight. So, I'm thinking to myself. I know he is not standing me up! Where is he? Finally, I called my friend and she says. Maybe he's at the other theater. I say. "Girl, what other theater?! She then tells me to walk and as I'm walking toward the theater. I see

Mark on the phone. We both start waving and
smiling at one another and we both hang up our
phones. Apparently, he was on the phone with his
Dad having him look for the paper with my number
on it. We missed the movie, but decided to get tickets
for another time. We then grabbed a bite to eat at
Olga's. So we are talking. Mark is a very
distinguished man and he is very handsome for his
age. As I'm gazing into his light brown eyes, I'm
thinking, "Why is this guy's feet, on top of my feet?"
I am appalled!

Please get your feet off my feet. What are you
doing? I felt violated. This was the weirdest,
creepiest thing I had ever experienced on a first date.
Oh No! This dude is weird, I can't. He told me that I
had pretty feet and that he could not resist. I was a bit
disturbed, but he was such a humorous person. I soon
forgot about the awkwardness of the moment. We
talked about our lives and our children. We still had
time before the movie so we walked to a nearby park
and sat and talked some more. Mark played tennis
and attended Tennessee State on a tennis scholarship.
He'd also been in the Air Force and later worked in
management for Continental Airlines. He loved jazz
and played chess. He was cool and funny, but still a
bit weird to me. We went to the movies and he
walked me to my car after our date. He thanked me
for going out with him and kissed me on the cheek.

The next day I talked to my friend Kelly about
him. She enlightened me. Girl he has culture, you
just haven't dated anyone with culture in a while. She
did admit that the foot incident was a bit weird
though. Mark and I just clicked. I loved hanging out

with him and vice versa. We had a whirlwind romance. He was so attentive and it had been a while since I had been with someone who cared about me and my son. I liked him but I needed my Grandma's opinion of him. So I took him by her house.

One evening, after one of our dates, the lights were dim in the house and my Grandma was resting on the couch in the living room. "Hi Grandma, I want you to meet my friend Mark." I said. "Come step into the light." She said. She shook his hand and stated that she could feel that he was a good person and got a good vibe from him. She loved the fact that he was older and established. She believed that I needed someone who was older and mature. So, when the Matriarch of my family approves, that's a good thing. Things were moving pretty quickly with Mark. He was all in and I liked him too. We went to the park one night and sat by the water. I knew that he was going to try and kiss me. He leaned in…His lips were soo soft.

Then I felt a little tongue. Umm, "No tongue, no tongue". Mark laughed. He was easy going very different from the other men that I had dated. As time progressed, we got closer and closer. Mark would call and say, "Am I going to see you today?" I really wasn't trying to be tied down. I didn't want a commitment. I had not too long ended things with Leonard and I enjoyed my freedom. As a matter of fact, Leonard called and tried to come by several times, but I wasn't interested. Eventually I told him about Mark and he demanded that I stop seeing him. I told him that I couldn't do that because Mark was too good to me. I mean it, "Get rid of him of now!" I told Leonard that he wasn't worth the risk. He was upset and he hung up on me. He then called back and asked if Mark and I had been intimate and I told him yes!! So, I thought that he would be so mad and that he would never want to speak to me again. I was mistaken. He told me that it didn't matter and to still get rid of Mark. I was shocked. It was over and Leonard knew it too.

I enjoyed being alone. I didn't want to complicate everything with a relationship. I was finally enjoying life. I was starting student teaching in the fall and my life had changed for the better. I expressed my feelings to Mark and told him that I just wanted to just have fun. Oh, so you're scared? No Mark, I'm not scared. Oh, so you're scared to be in a relationship with me? No, I'm not scared Mark. Should I be scared? Well what if I dared you to be. What if I dare you to be in a relationship with me? I thought that was the silliest thing that I had ever heard. What are you talking about? I giggled. It was funny. Okay! I'm not scared. I said, "Don't dare me now, I may take you up on that."

Before the phone call was over, we were together. Mark told me that he wasn't playing any games with me and that he wanted to settle down. Every time I saw Mark he was getting down on one knee and asking me to marry him. "Mark what are you doing?" I love you, "Will you marry me?" Mark look, stop joking. Please stop playing, you are so silly. No, I'm serious. I want you to be my wife. This went on frequently. Needless to say, I didn't take him serious. Then it happened. One day he did it again. He got down on one knee and asked me to marry him. It was

something about the way that he asked this time, that made me know that he was serious. I knew that I loved him, but I had been hurt so much, I wasn't going to pressure anyone into wanting me. He repeated it and I said, "Are you serious?"
He said yes, "I'm serious, will you marry me?"
I looked into his eyes and I said, "No you're not, you blinked twice."
"Blinked twice, oh Lord what are you talking about?" He laughed so hard at me. "Woman, you have a lot of issues. I am not those other men. I love you and I want you to marry me and be my wife." I smiled, looked him in his eyes and said yes. The following week we went looking for rings. I was so excited and happy. I knew this man really loved me. I felt his love every time I was in his presence. I was on a cloud. My son and I were finally with someone who loved us and wanted to build a family. The day he bought my engagement ring was epic. I was absolutely elated. The ring was beautiful and when he put it on my finger, I could have melted. I have to tell my Grandma. I could not stop looking at my ring as we rode to my Grandmother's house. "Baby, pay attention to the road." Mark said. I was driving and kept looking at my ring.

When we arrived at Grandma's house, everyone was standing outside. My brother and cousins. I rode up flashing my ring. "I'm engaged. The first thing my brother Mari says is, "Does Grandma know?" No, we're about to tell her now. Aw Man, I can't miss this. I got to see this. Everyone thought that my Grandma would be upset. I wasn't even sure how she would respond. I was hopeful though. Grandma was very happy. I showed her my ring and she smiled. She was very happy for Mark and me. She knew that I had been through so much with Gino and being a single mother. She was happy that I finally had someone in my life that loved me and wanted to be a father to my son. Not everyone in my family was happy about my engagement though. Some thought that we were moving much too fast. My friend Kelly was very concerned and thought that Mark was a rebound from Leonard. This was so far from the truth. I had been praying for the Lord to send me my husband. I had been confessing and believing God for him to manifest in our lives. Yes, it was a fast engagement. But when you know what you want it doesn't take years to act on it.

I went to church and Bishop saw that there were some changes that were around me. He said that I was about to make a major decision and to be prayerful. He asked if that made any sense to me and I told him yes. After service, I told him that Mark had proposed to me. He wanted to meet him. They met and Bishop asks him numerous questions regarding me and my son. Mark admitted that he had been previously married and that he made some mistakes in that marriage. He respected Mark's openness in regard to accountability. We had both made a lot of mistakes and wanted to get it right this time.

My father wasn't in my life. I had not seen him since my Granddaddy died. I did have a male authority in my life. So that's why I met with Bishop. Mark didn't really understand it. He wasn't familiar with spiritual protocol. I explained to him the significance of the meeting. Although, I had already accepted the engagement proposal, I still wanted The Man of God to meet him. Some may question why I accepted before the meeting. I accepted his proposal because I did have a relationship with God for myself. I knew what I felt in my heart and I knew the kind of man I believed God for. To be perfectly honest. I didn't want a man who was in the church all day. I still liked to have fun and enjoy life. I loved adventure and laughter. I wanted balance. Yes, I believe in God and I have a relationship with him. He loves me in all my mess. Does he want me in the mess? No, he doesn't, he wants me to be whole. I was still a work in progress.

I had dated someone who quoted scriptures all day and practically lived at the church, but he still wasn't the one. I was looking for confirmation. One word of warning and I would have had to rethink the whole thing. But I didn't get that. He gave us his blessing and that was enough for me. My Grandmother, the leaders in the church, some family and a few close friends knew that I was engaged. I informed those individuals that were important to me. We were married in November 2005 at a chapel in Farmington Hills. Joyce and her husband were our witnesses.

This Marriage was not a fairytale marriage. Both of us were married before, so there were some adjustments. He had two children in his previous marriage. Two teenage girls that lived in Ohio. He saw them often and made sure he paid his child support. I loved the fact that he was in their lives and cared for them financially. We were a blended family. Everything was wonderful in the beginning.

We were excited and doing things as a family. We planned a cruise and I was ecstatic. I had never been on an airplane before. My first time was with my new husband. It was exhilarating and I was happy with my new life. We went to the Bahamas and Grandma watched Chris so that we could have a little honeymoon. I called constantly, until she finally said "Girl aren't you supposed to be on a trip. Well enjoy yourself, Chris is fine." I finally relaxed and had fun. It was memorable. I loved the cruise and we had a wonderful time. I was happy and enjoying myself in a good way.

I got along with his family too. His mother welcomed me and his father was cool. They embraced us and loved my son as their own grandchild. My life seemed to be finally coming together. The first 9 months were great, and then we had some turbulence. My husband was older, so he was set in his ways. I was always very domineering, so we clashed a little bit. Dating is different than marriage. Mark had issues from his past that was starting to surface. Most of his issues dealt with his temper. He was always laughing and joking and just easy going, but when he got mad he was mad. I also was very feisty and temperamental. This was a very bad combination.

In the beginning, getting to know one another, everything was sweet and innocent, but as time progressed things started to change. I could not let go of some of my old habits, I liked to go out from time to time. It wasn't often, but I did. This was a problem for Mark. He loved the fact that I was in church and a quote, unquote, good girl. Although, I went to church. I had not been delivered. I was lukewarm. I still liked to hang out with the sinners. I hadn't totally surrendered to God. Even after all those years of strife and depression. I still hadn't fled from sin. Most of my family was not in the church and the ones that were, still partied. It was very comfortable, because there was no one to hold me accountable. There wasn't anyone to judge me. Though, deep down I was convicted. I would suppress it though. Because it was easier to conform. I would get together with my friends who weren't married and still hang out. This became an issue in our marriage.

I had come from a dominating family of women so having my way was a must. Again, I didn't know how to keep quiet. So, when he would express his feelings, I would go off. I hadn't learned that every battle isn't mine to win. I loved drama because that was all I knew. There were several incidents where we would argue like cats and dogs. I felt that he wanted to control me. Mark came from a family of discipline. His parents were married and then divorced. His father was a marine and His mother worked and retired from the bank. He is a man of business and order. He is very good about the fundamentals of life, such as credit worthiness, paying bills on time and saving money. I didn't grow up learning about savings, checking accounts and building credit. I grew up learning how to survive and that I should spend money.

Most of my family lived paycheck to paycheck and that was the normal. So, Mark and I clashed in the first years of our marriage over finances. It was a tremendous struggle when it came to those life lessons. Mark is definitely an Alpha Male and I am an Alpha Female. We both were relentless in proving each other wrong. We also had some personality challenges. Mark is an introvert and keeps his emotions inside. He's not really comfortable with expressing himself. I on the other hand, will always tell you how I feel. You will definitely hear it even if you don't want to hear it. I'm going to tell you anyway. This made our lives difficult sometimes. Those first seven years. My God!!! We had some good times as well, but at times it was challenging.

Mark tried to go to church with me, but he wasn't feeling it. I knew that I had yet again married someone who loved God, but didn't care for my church. This put a heavy strain on our marriage. I was in church and dancing in the dance ministry. Yes I went back. I went to rehearsals and we had to dance every week. I even went out of town to Ohio and Atlanta to dance for conferences. Dance was always my passion and the ministry had changed. It was under new leadership. Sister Nakia was the new leader so it was a blessing to be a part of this group. I built some strong friendships and sisterhood in this ministry.

It was different from when I was there before. I ministered in dance for years. I admit although I was content, my husband wasn't because it took me away from home. He wasn't there with me. So he didn't have the connection I did, to the church. I went about everything wrong and I take accountability for my actions. Before we were married, we were in sin. I knew that I was wrong because I had sowed a seed of lust into the marriage. Mark is very passionate and so am I. Was I wrong, yes I was. I wanted what I wanted. I tried on several occasions to tell him that I could not live that way. I was selfish because I could have really led him to God, but I allowed lust and flesh to keep me from being a true witness to him. Mark, like me, hadn't grown up in the church. He did attend and even went to the altar. A part of me thinks he did it for me. He would deny though. I knew his heart and I knew in my heart that he loved me. I also knew that he needed some things to be delivered from as well. Things from his past, his childhood and his first marriage. I knew that he desired to be loved just like I did. We both yearned to make the wrongs right in our lives. We had good intentions, but needed God to bring it to fruition.

We both needed deliverance at the time and I didn't see it. We did fall in love with one another for a reason. There is good and bad in everyone. A person has to want to be good. We all have the potential to be good, but it is a choice. It's called free will. There are qualities that I truly love about Mark. He can be the most supportive and wonderful person and believe that God sent him to love me and to be a father to my son. He taught him how to eat at the table with utensils and has assisted me in his educational and daily functional skills. He reminds me often to focus on Christian's abilities and not his disabilities. The Lord had brought someone in my life that puts his family first, loves me unconditionally, and who loves my son as his own child. My breakthrough for Christian truly manifested. Bishop laid hands on Christian in his office. He prayed for God to rejuvenate and restore those brain cells that were destroyed at birth. God gave me a miracle. It didn't happen all of sudden. It was gradual. It was about 6 months later.

God was beginning to deliver and heal me from the past as well. I knew in my heart when I began to walk in Christ wholeheartedly, that He would heal my son. I needed to be able to stand in the gap, pray and most of all believe that I was worthy for Him to do this. I had to really forgive myself. Before, I really didn't believe that God had forgiven me for my sins and disobedience. The devil is cunning. For years he whispered in my ear and told me that I wasn't worthy, and say to me why would God heal my son? I would hear you're not this and you're not that, but the devil is a liar. I had to come to the realization that God does love me. Jesus died for my sins. I'm redeemed and covered by his blood and I'm a joint heir of Jesus Christ. After making the decision and doing what God had called me to do, that's when the blessings came. God healed my son.

Christian started talking. I received a call from his teacher. He was attending school in Southfield. Christian's teacher believed that he had autistic characteristics. Here we go again with this diagnosis. Finally, I decided to have the tests done again. He was placed in an autistic self-contained classroom. After about 2 months in the class. I receive a call from his teacher. "Christian said his ABC"s today" There was a long pause. "HELLO" Did you hear me? "Christian said his ABC"s today." I stared at the phone. I couldn't believe it. Yet, I did believe. She informed me to have him say them when he got home that day. GOD is FAITHFUL!! He says "Mama", recites his alphabets, can count to 100, spell, write his first and last name, and make requests. God is so awesome!!! Things seemed to be turning around in my life, then I got the phone call.

It was June 29, 2006 and everyone was at my house celebrating Christian's birthday. I get a phone call and it's from the police department. I'm sorry to call you to inform of this, but your father Wayne is dead. My daddy is dead? Yes, your father is dead. Tears started streaming down my face. It had been a couple of years since I talked to him. He was still in his lifestyle and because I was trying to have a different life and raise Chris in a more stable environment with less drama and chaos. I decided I couldn't have my dad be a part of my life, knowing that he was still using drugs. I was going the tough love route. And those that have done that know that sometimes you win in the situation and sometimes you don't.

My father didn't have a chance to come out of it because he was found shot in his leg in a house. I was told that it appeared the person was not trying to kill him, but when he was shot in the leg that the bullet hit an artery and he bled to death. They believe that it was a crack house and he died alone. I was trying to keep my composure because like I said it was Christian's birthday. I guess he had died maybe three days before and they were trying to find next of kin. They were able to find me. We were all here having a party for my son. As I began to tell everyone what happened. I broke down crying. A lot of it was guilt and regret because I didn't have a chance to really have a real relationship with my father. And that bothered me. It ate me up. It tore the core of me. With my mom, it was different. She was always with me. I saw her every day. She was with me all the time. We had our talks throughout my life. My dad and I really didn't have the opportunity to connect the way that I've always wanted too. So, his death really depressed me and then on top of that, there was no insurance. There was no family that could assist with finances because everyone had passed away. My Grandparents were gone. So, not only did I have to deal with his death, I had to go identify his body at the morgue and also bury him. My husband was so gracious and dressed him in one of his suits. I had to put together a funeral and it was very hard for me. Daddy, I love you, continue to rest in peace because you fought a hard battle. You were addicted to these drugs for years, years and finally you can have some sort of peace. I hope you are at peace. I pray you are at peace.

After a year of marriage, I became pregnant. My husband was excited about the news. Everyone thought that he was crazy starting over and having another child, but I believe he did it for me. He was fully aware of my desire to have another child. He also wanted to have another chance to be in the home and raise his child. It was a second chance for the both of us to have a real family. We immediately started researching Obstetricians that specialized in high risk pregnancies and we found one. I started prenatal care immediately. I knew that it would be a journey, but we were standing on the word of God. Early on in my pregnancy after dancing at church, I started to spot. I was in the dressing room and my dance leader and friend Nakia came to the back and asked to pray for me. "How did you know?" I asked her. "I just knew." She responded. She laid hands on my stomach and prayed for my baby. She also suggested that I go to Dr. Beverly and ask her to pray. I didn't want to be a burden to anyone, but she assured me that this was too important to not say anything. Dr. Beverly prayed and laid hands on my stomach. She prayed that I would not miscarry, that the baby would stay in the womb and that I would deliver a full term healthy baby. I had to be on complete bed rest for my pregnancy. I prayed daily and meditated on the word along with reading a wonderful book entitled Supernatural Childbirth. I also received a cerclage which is a stitch to keep the cervix from dilating. A family friend that had the same condition advised me to contact this Specialist. His name was Dr. Blessed and I knew that was a divine connection.

Mark and I consulted with Dr. Blessed and he told me that I had to reach 14 weeks before they could put in the cerclage. So I had to get through the first trimester in order to even have the cerclage. I had to stand on faith. My husband never left my side during the procedure. Mark was stable, strong, and reliable. I could depend on him to be there for me. I had to receive progesterone shots every week in my buttocks and could not do any strenuous walking or exercise. I bled all through my pregnancy and had to take several trips through emergency while carrying my daughter. I'm talking bright red blood. God had her covered and shielded. The enemy wanted to snatch her, but God covered her. Mark was there for me the entire pregnancy. It was totally different from when I was pregnant with Christian. There was no stress or me wondering where my husband was. He came home straight from work every day and made sure my needs were met. Bringing me home cheese burgers with chili fries. I craved that and ice cream. He was patient and understanding because there was no intimacy after the cerclage. So for about 6 months we couldn't be intimate. Anything I needed, he made sure that I had it. I was finally happy.

The day I gave birth was so exciting. The night before I had a slight headache and was anxious. It was a hot summer night in July. Mark and I slept at the foot of the bed with his arms wrapped around me. The next day we went in for a scheduled cesarean and our daughter, my second miracle baby was born. He held my hand the entire time as our baby girl came into the world. The doctor put her in his arms you could see the love in his eyes. She looked like a little Chinese baby. Mark told me that he had strong genes, but geesh. She didn't look anything like me. Everything was perfect in our world. We had her dedicated at the church and our families came to witness her being dedicated to the Lord. Mark had started coming back to church with me. It was an adjustment having this little baby in the home.

Christian was so accustomed to it being the two of us. I had to transition him into this new family as well. I was happy and had my family. The fall of 2007 brought a lot of tragedy into our lives. My Great Aunt Evelyn, my Grandmother's youngest sister, lost her battle to cancer and in the following month we lost my Aunt Bunnie, my Grandmother's daughter.

My Great Aunt was a paralegal; she was smart, funny and loved jazz. My Aunt Bunnie who had suffered with addiction for years was diagnosed with COPD. She died the same month. She was on a respirator for two weeks and I refused to let her go. My Grandmother knew that she wasn't coming back to us, but I was hoping for a miracle. Our family felt helpless as we witnessed her organs began to shut down. I prayed. I cried I laid hands on her. I didn't want to let my Aunt go. I asked God to allow her to wake up so that she could receive Jesus Christ as her Lord and Savior. She opened her eyes. She had a tube inside her throat so she couldn't talk.

I prayed the prayer of salvation and I asked her to use her eyes as a form of communication. I requested that she blink once for yes and twice for no. I asked a couple of questions to make sure that she understood what I requested of her. I asked her did she repent of her sins and accept Jesus Christ as her Lord and Savior. She blinked once for Yes. I knew in my heart she is in heaven. I was heartbroken. I was very close to my Aunt Bunnie. She would keep us laughing and she was so humorous. There was never a dull moment when she was around. I would try to talk to her about her lifestyle and she would get mad and tell me that I was the niece and that she wasn't going to listen to me. I would fuss sometimes because I wanted her to get delivered. She loved God, she told me that she wanted to be delivered she said she just didn't know how to do it. That she wasn't strong enough. I knew her heart and that she was a loving caring person who loved her mother, children and her family. Rest in peace Auntie.

Love Nots

No Fairytale, It's Work

11.

Rediscovering Me!

As the years passed, things were good. Laura brings Mark and I so much joy. I always knew if I had a little girl, that I would name her after my mom. She is a very smart little girl and had an old soul. She is definitely daddy's little girl and they have a beautiful bond. My step-daughters who were in their 20's was adjusting to having a little sister. It was tough for them in the beginning. Because it had always been the two of them and here was this little sister. Laura was the stability that I needed because after the season of carrying her, it changed me. I now had my two miracle children. She slowed me all the way down because she was hyper. Therefore, she and Chris kept me busy. Mark and I tried attending church again together as a family. It wasn't long before he'd stop going. That made our lives difficult, because I was trying to change. I needed more of a spiritual connection and I wanted to grow in ministry. I was beginning to have many prophetic dreams and God was beginning to use me in these dreams. God was revealing things to me regularly and it was drawing me more and more. I was receiving prophecies every time a prophet came to the church. I was getting called out sometimes sitting in the back of the sanctuary or my name was being called out to receive a Word. Prophecies about my calling and things that God was going to do in my life, as well as my family through my obedience. There was so much occurring in the years to follow that would distract me from obtaining those goals.

My Uncle Bud, my Grandma's brother, passed away to cancer in 2010. It was very hurtful to our family. Uncle Bud was also a giver and he always made sure that whenever he came, he had gifts to bear. He also loved to play baseball and he was known for that. We gave him a beautiful memorial in honor of his life. I eventually graduated in December 2013 with a Bachelor's of Science degree in elementary education with a major in special education from Wayne State University. I was the first in my immediate family to receive a Bachelor's degree and my plans are to continue my education. This was a major accomplishment for me. I know my mother wanted me to get a degree, so I know that she is smiling from heaven and proud of me.

Although I was married, I struggled a lot emotionally. We went through a very trying season. I had a lot of loss in my family over the years. My uncle John died in March of 2016. He had battled diabetes and also his addiction to crack for years. Grandma and I pleaded with him to stop, but he didn't listen. Ultimately, he lost his life. The family was devastated. He was my Grandmother's only son. His death really impacted me, because I really tried to talk to him. I tried to be there for him and when he died he thought that I was upset with him. I was guilt-ridden. After losing my Uncle, our marriage shifted. We went through a very hard trial last year.

The marriage vow states to leave mother and father and cleave to your wife. Married couples should cleave to one another. I had not done that. I still took on the responsibility of my family. I was really burdened with things that I should not have been burdened with. As a result, my marriage suffered. I put everyone and everything before God and my household. The marriage was strained so my husband turned to someone else.

He met her on social media. It started with innocent flirting, chatting in the inbox and liking too many pictures. This inappropriate behavior turned into an affair. You have to be careful with social media. You have access to all types of women and men at your fingertips. People are using these platforms such as Facebook, Twitter and Instagram for instant attention and gratification. Everyone wants to be liked. Hey look at me. Look at what I'm doing. Look at my picture. Like my picture. If I don't get any likes, I must not be funny, I must not be pretty. We determine our value based on a thumb up emoji. This adulterous relationship slipped in right under my nose. I had no clue. My husband played games on the computer, so it wasn't unusual for him to be on late at night. I made the mistake of assuming he was content. He was always a homebody so I didn't suspect a thing. I was a busybody, trying to save everyone but my husband. I felt as if I had to do it. Everyone called me, my grandma, my brothers, my cousins. It was all so exhausting. By the time I got home there wasn't anything left for my family. Everyone pulled on me. If there were an emergency they called me. Sometimes I got calls at 2:00 in the morning and I would leave my bed to break up an argument and drama with my family at my Grandma's house.

My husband would beg me not to leave, but I told him I had too… that was my family. If there was a crisis, they would call *me*. I had become mentally and physically drained. I had become my mother. She was the fixer and I had become the fixer. This went on for years…. I became my family's savior.

As my husband was building an attachment with another woman and I didn't have a clue until it was too late. I knew something had changed in him. He was dressing a little younger, wearing his Adidas track suits with his hat to the back. Always looking in the mirror and became very obsessed with working out.

He was pulling in the driveway with music that I believed a 50 something year old man should not be listening too. Drake, Future and even J Cole. I assumed that he was adjusting to getting older and perhaps just going through a midlife crisis. Shoot, I was adjusting to getting older myself. I was diagnosed with hypertension and now had to take high blood pressure medication every day. I had two procedures for fibroids and eventually had to get a partial hysterectomy. So, I had issues too. He was diagnosed with diabetes a few years ago. He almost had a diabetic stroke at work. He didn't even know that he was sick. We had to rush him to the hospital because his blood sugar was almost 900. My husband went on insulin and had to take a shot 4 times a day. I worked with him, I prayed for him. I laid hands on him and I made a commitment to cook healthy meals for him daily. I have made his lunch almost every day since he was diagnosed with diabetes. I did that because I love him. Because of my care, God's grace and Mark's diligence, he was able to get off the four shots of insulin a day, to just taking a pill a day.

I stuck with him. For better or for worse for richer or for poorer and in sickness or in health. Yes, those are the vows. People just say them without really thinking about those words. They are powerful. For better or for worse. What's the worse? Is the worse that your husband could break the marriage covenant? That your husband could break the agreement? You can stay or you can leave. The decision is based on that couple and their individual circumstance. God will give you grounds for divorce. That's the Word! If your spouse commits adultery, you my dear are free to leave. I left Gino because of his adultery! I divorced Gino in a heartbeat, but I was 26 years old when I was married the first time. We had no business even getting married in the first place. This time around was supposed to be different. This was my soul mate. We were really in Love, in grown folk's love.

We were both divorced previously and had experienced the breakdown of a family. We were both older and mature and should have gotten our wild days out of our system. I believed in my heart that this man loved me and that he loved the air I breathe. It was earth shattering and I wanted to hurt him as badly as he hurt me. I was once again broken. I thought that story in my life was over. I put him on such a pedestal. He could never do this to me, not him. I was so hurt because Mark knew what I had experienced in my previous relationships. He knew how I was betrayed and cheated on. Yet, he did this to me. How do I keep making the same choices and choosing the same kind of men?

Sin is sin and it all started with fornication. That is the gateway sin. It opens the door to everything else. It is the door that opens to destruction. Learn from my lessons. God wants you to be whole and happy. I realized that Mark was flawed. He pleaded and asked me for forgiveness. He expressed that he realized that he was wrong and he repented to God and me. I didn't want to forgive him. I was angry, full of resentment and wanted revenge. I wanted him to suffer. I wanted him to feel empty inside and to feel the pain and the humiliation and hurt that I felt. I handed him the eviction notice. I wanted him out of the home. We were living a lie. He had to get out! Leave! I didn't care where he went, but I could no longer look at him.

My daughter was distraught. She could hear her parents arguing. We tried to be discreet but it was tearing our family apart. She would run in the room crying begging us to stop arguing. I was pissed and a part of me hated him for destroying our beautiful family. How could he do this to us? My mother and daddy were not married, but their relationship almost destroyed me. It created such a spirit of hurt and rejection over me that followed me into my teenage and young adult years. My daughter was not supposed to go through what I went through. We failed her! We failed her!

It was time for me to take responsibility for my part in it. I put everything and everyone before my husband and my household. I remember him asking, when birthday parties and events would come up, if we could go as a couple. He stated that I was not the chauffeur for my family. I would say, well you know they need me to drive. Well baby, can you make the exception and have someone else drive your family this time? I wouldn't do it. He would always back out and stay home with the children. He told me there were times he felt like he was just the babysitter.

I must admit most events he was not in attendance. Not because he didn't want to go, but who would care for the children if we both attended. It was hard. That part I will take responsibility for. I should have never put my family before him. I love my family with all my heart, but God gave me a husband and I should have honored him more and cleaved to him. We have gone on two trips as a couple since we have been married. Both trips were before Laura was born and Laura will be ten this summer. So in 12 years we have been on a trip twice. We would get out occasionally. My Grandmother would watch them so that we could have a night way for our Anniversary or Valentine's Day. Other than that, it really wasn't much time for us to sow into our relationship. I see how things manifested, but it still was no excuse for his behavior. He sinned and so did

I. This situation on top of losing my uncle John brought me to my knees. It brought me back to God!!

You see God is a jealous God. No one should come before Him. I had put everything and everybody before Him. I had forgotten who blessed me. I had forgotten who was there when Christian was born. Who gave me the home, the cars? God! Who blessed me? God. My husband absolutely adored me and for him to do this to me was shocking, but he had also lost his way. I never dreamed he would do this to me. Not me. What made him exempt? He's not Jesus. Only Jesus is the perfect one, The Anointed One. We are flesh and this flesh is filthy, it's dirty. We are flawed individuals, that need the revelation of the true living God. Wait Now! Let me reiterate. I'm not excusing his behavior, not at all. He was wrong, dead wrong. He committed adultery and it took me months to forgive him.

God said in order for you to heal you are going to have to forgive him. "Lord he did this to me, how could he hurt me and our children this way?" I cried. God told me you should have never made him your God! I'm your comforter, your peace and I'm Jehovah Jireh your provider. You have always put a man before me. You have always put others before me. How many times have I showed up for you? How many times have I been there for you? You've always put a man before me. I'm the key to your wholeness. I'm the key to your happiness. You will never find that in a man. I am your God! I had to get back on my knees. These things happened to me to connect me back to my Heavenly Father. Life is a journey and we have choices in life. I chose to forgive my husband. Ultimately, he is a good man and a good father. He works every day and takes care of his family. That is the core of who he is. That's why we stayed together. He cried every night and fought for our marriage and our family. I stayed with the understanding that this can never happen again. Was I completely innocent throughout these 12 years No! I had a couple of incidents where I behaved inappropriately.

For example, I stopped by David's house to inform him of my Aunt Bunnie's death. My husband was not aware of this visit. I know that's not the same, but I didn't tell him that I saw my ex. Let alone went to his house. I also had conversations when an ex has called me. Some of these conversations my husband wasn't even aware of. This has not been easy. We are taking it literally one day at a time. I'm saying God, you have to be in this because it's not going to work if you're not in it. I want to trust him wholeheartedly again, but once the trust is broken it takes work to get it back. It takes the presence of the Holy Spirit. I'm trusting God to save my husband. He told me to stay and I believe it is for a reason. I believe in us and I believe in our love and I believe in our family. So much was lost. It's not going to happen overnight. Just like it took time to get to this point. It's going to take time to rebuild the trust and to rebuild the respect again. But I have faith and I'm going to hold on to that. Even when the devil tries to trick me and make me believe that all of this was in vain. Not only was this man my best friend, he was my confidant and he is not only my husband he's my brother in Christ and I care for his soul. I'm praying that he becomes the man that God has called him to be. It's up to him to choose to be better. Not for me or for our family, but for himself. He is my daughter's father and I will always want the best for him.

12.

Self-Love

When you don't have self-love, you open yourself up to wolves in sheep clothing. They can see you. They can smell you. They know when you have low self-esteem. They know when you're desperate, by the way you dress and the way that you present yourself. Don't get me wrong, women can be sexy. You're allowed to be sexy, you're allowed to own your sexuality and own the fact that you're a woman. It's when you overdo it, that it can be a problem. When you see nothing but breast and you know that dress is too tight or that shirt is too tight you've gone too far. That was me. I dressed very provocatively because I wanted attention. When I look back on my life, I clearly see that I didn't love myself *and* I didn't value myself. I put on a good front and was a good actress. I presented myself as if I had it all together.

I pretended like I didn't need a man. I don't need anybody. I love myself. I had all the clichés memorized. It was all an act and those wolves out there saw right through it. Because they target women that are deeply insecure, needy and desperate. They say, she wants me to believe she's all that but she isn't! I'm going to break her all the way down and show her just how much she's worth. I've had men tell me that. Some of them admitted it. Yeah, I saw you and you were just so puffed up and I said to myself that I just had to break you down. Why would a man want to break a woman down that he knows is already broken?

Anytime you're the loudest one in the group and always need to be seen, you are over compensating for something. You are pretending to be confident because you know that you are really insecure. Real confidence doesn't act unseemly and does not have to convince anyone of their confidence…they just are! Because I lacked self-love, I didn't really know who I was in God. Although I was told that God loves me, I still hadn't really experienced His love yet. Simply because I was pursuing men instead of really pursuing Him. After some time had passed, I was right back into sin, because I really didn't know how to pursue God. I didn't know that I had to give in this relationship. I've heard that all my life. God loves everybody.

God loves the sinner. People say they love you and will betray and mistreat you. I've had family members that say they love me and have treated me like crap. That have treated me like there wasn't an ounce of blood anywhere and at times treated me like an enemy. I could go on and on I could write a chapter on that alone. But God is Love, better described as Agape Love. He loves you no matter what! Before I was formed in my mother's belly, God knew me. He sanctified me and He loved me, He knew I was going to go through all of that. But He wanted me to come to the revelation on my own of who He was in my life, a faithful loving God. I went through those trials. I went through those horrendous, ridiculous relationships, but they were lessons and I needed to go through that. I needed to know who I was. I needed to stand boldly, the woman that I am today and know clearly that God is with me. As long as God is with me, I can stand against any man that is against me.

So, I had to go through those experiences. Yes, it was very hurtful. Yes, I felt alone. Yes, I felt abused. But I have to take some responsibility because of my behavior. I didn't present myself as a young lady. I didn't present myself as a woman who was trying to build a relationship with God. I presented myself as a woman that you could have sex with. I'm being very honest with myself and being very transparent about that. I went into the majority of those situations knowing, looking, and searching for someone to love me. Because I didn't love myself. I put up a good front though.

I knew how to bat my eyelashes and walk a certain way. I knew how to say and do things to appear cute and adorable. I was always very feisty and sassy and some men love that. I truly didn't know who I was. I didn't know the real me. I didn't know that I was God's daughter and that he had a man that he wanted to send to me that would love me for who I am. That would love me in all my quirkiness and my craziness. I've heard that my entire life. Girl you are so crazy. No, I'm not crazy. I just have a sense of humor and I love to make others laugh. I have a very loud and boisterous laugh and God wanted to send me someone who would appreciate and love that laugh. I didn't know that there was somebody who would love me for me and that would accept me for me.

I felt that I had to dress provocative and act a certain way to get attention and in the end, I always loss. I always ended up somewhere heartbroken, with my heart in the gutter. If you don't get anything from me sharing my experiences, get this. If you find yourself always choosing the same type of men and always getting your heart broken all the time, it's something that you are doing, that's drawing these types of men. You need to change the way you present yourself. You need to change your conversation. You need to change your mindset. When your mind doesn't change, you will repeat your mistakes. Oh, yes you will. I was a repeat offender. I have gone through hell, back and through hell again, and I'm only standing because of God's grace. It could have been worse. I'm grateful, but **you do have to look at yourself**.

If you're presenting yourself as someone who is promiscuous, with your cleavage out all the time and clothes so tight that you can see every dimple in your butt, you are going to attract men who just want to have sex with you. They're not going to see the sustenance in you because you have not discovered it yet. Once you discover your real value, you will not resort to cheap tricks and tawdry seductions. Men who are looking for a woman who values herself, will not choose you and the ones that do choose you won't want a serious relationship with you. They will use you for the sex that you so easily offer and give them. Your desperation for love is the bait and once you give in, they will use you and abuse you, until they are tired of you or become bored. Then they are on to the next woman, the next girl. I had to go through those things. They were lessons, but you know what, my daughter will not go through what I went though. No! I am here to teach her, to talk to her and affirm her and share my story. She has a father who is in her life who loves her and affirms her and builds up her self-esteem. She's a daddy's girl.

I didn't have a daddy. I didn't have a father. My father loved me. Yeah, he loved me, but we didn't have a real relationship. By the time I was an adult, we tried to connect but it was too late. We tried to build a relationship, but there was a disconnection because he wasn't there when I was a little girl. So I missed out on all the affirmations, conversations and warnings about boys and men. I missed out on that.

My self-esteem was so low. If I had a daddy to build me up—the first joker that came to me talking game, would have been shut down immediately! I would have run. I mean literally ran from those dudes. I wouldn't have thought... Oh, I can change him. Oh, I can make him love me. Oh, he's just a bad boy that needs a good woman. Oh, girl, I don't know why he's out here with these women. He knows he loves me. That's Nonsense! That's Foolishness! I actually use to say these things. The curse is broken with me. The curse stops with me.

I was saved, but I stayed in a backslidden state for years. God couldn't bless me the way that he wanted to bless me. I still hadn't been delivered from the residue and the stench of the world. My mindset had not changed. Years later, forever in rewind, repeating the mistakes of my family. Yes, I am married. I have been married for 12 years but a seed of fornication was sown into my marriage and that thing that was sowed came back and bite me. I wasn't delivered when I met my husband. There was residue still there. That lust spirit was still there. It hovers over you and will have you in bondage and all tangled up. I just thank God that I was able to get out of that mindset and get free.

Once we were married I wanted to be the good little Christian wife. I wanted to live holy and I expected him to change and conform, but that seed of lust and fornication had already been planted. It tried to destroy us. God's Grace is sufficient. I had to repent as recent as last year for that. God brought

233

it all back to my remembrance and he showed me. ME. Last year I rededicated my life back to Christ. That Generational curse in my bloodline is broken In Jesus Name. When I got serious about my walk with God, it was on. I made a vow that I would never put anything or anyone before God again. I am back in fellowship with God and other believers. I spend time with God. I have connected to two powerful prayer lines and I am taking it one day at a time. I'm enjoying spending time with my heavenly Father. Yes, my husband and I are taking it one day at a time. I finally know who I am. I love myself.

I'm not flawless, but I'm learning more about the Word. I'm learning about myself in God's word. I'm Me! I'm Me! I celebrate ME now. I can celebrate my flaws and all. I wouldn't be standing today the way that I'm standing strong, if I didn't know God. Knowing that He loves me. If I had not gone through those lessons, I wouldn't have this testimony that God could heal, deliver and bless you. Love Nots! Yes, I believe there were some people that I believe truly loved me and then there were some who didn't love me at all and then they were some, who just didn't know how to love me. Simply because they didn't love themselves. So how can you love someone if you don't love yourself? You can't, that's just it. Especially if you don't have a revelation of who you are. Most of these men didn't even know who they were, they didn't have fathers. They didn't have a father to mentor them or to show them what a real man is. God is the Father I never had and He can be your Father too, if you will let Him.

When we study God's Word, establish a prayer life and begin to have a relationship with Him, He will reveal, the true you and He will reveal His love. His love will shower down on you. And then you can be the man or woman that God has called you to be. Then you can be equally yoked with someone and live happily. Not perfect because nothing is perfect, but, we can be whole and happy within ourselves. Isn't that what everyone is searching for any way, Love? Everyone wants to be loved. God so loved the world that He gave His only begotten Son for our sins. He loved us that much! Because He knew we were a mess. We are a Mess. This thing called life is a day to day walk. It's a journey and we are supposed to learn from each other.

Why did I write this book? I wrote this book so that someone can learn from my experiences and learn what not to do. Oh my! She went through that! Oh no, I don't want to go through that. I need to shut that down. Wow! That guy did what to her? Ok once, twice, and thrice and she still stayed thinking things would change. You will say, "Oh no, that's not for me." So if you see the signs and the red flags and you find yourself repeating the same patterns, exit stage left! Back out gracefully and remind yourself that God loves you and wants something better for you and that you deserve better. Today my life looks drastically different. I need it to be known that I have not only forgiven myself for my mistakes and the role I played in all of my heartache but I have also forgiven my father, all the men I was in relationships with and even my stepfather Charles.

I am currently working in substitute teaching which I find very rewarding. Pouring into children's lives and assisting with their education. I also started an organization for parents with children that have special needs called Chosen Hearts. This organization was formed to let parents know that they are not alone and to build empathy and understanding within the community by bridging the gap with awareness. What the devil meant for my demise and destruction, God made a blessing. He is so merciful and is truly a God of second, third, fourth chances etc... I'm nothing without Him. I thank Him for the miraculous manifestations of blessings in my life. I have a stronger, more personal relationship with Him and I honor Him daily. I praise God for what He's done and what He's continuing to do in my family. He has created in me a tenacious spirit and vitality for life. He is my source, my peace and my strength. These lessons have sincerely humbled me and I know that God's love is everlasting. It's eternal!

Love Nots

237

Self-Love

Salvation and Rededication

John 3:16

For God so loved the world, that he gave his only begotten Son, that whosoever believeth in him should not perish, but have everlasting life.

Romans 10:9 &10

That if thou shalt confess with thy mouth the Lord Jesus, and shall believe in thine heart that God hath raise him from the dead, thou shalt be saved.

For with the heart man believeth unto righteousness; and with the mouth confession is made into salvation.

Salvation Prayer

Father, I come to You in the Name of Jesus. Your Word says, 'Whosoever shall call on the name of the Lord shall be saved' (Acts 2:21). I am calling on You. I pray and ask Jesus to come into my heart and

238

be Lord over my life according to Romans 10:9-10: 'If thou shalt confess with thy mouth the Lord Jesus, and shalt believe in thine heart that God has raised him from the dead, thou shalt be saved. For with the heart man believeth unto righteousness; and with the mouth confession is made unto salvation.' I do that now. I confess that Jesus is Lord, and I believe in my heart that God raised Him from the dead. I am now reborn! I am a Christian, a child of Almighty God! I am saved! In Jesus Name. Amen!

Rededication Prayer

Father, in the name of Jesus, your Word says if we confess our sins, you are faithful and just to forgive us our sins and to cleanse us from all unrighteousness (1 John 1:9). I confess my sins, and I thank you for your forgiveness and cleansing me. Father, I desire a closer walk with you and I rededicate my spirit, my mind, my heart and my body back to you. I ask for a fresh anointing, upon my whole life. I thank you for the Blood of Jesus, which continually cleanse me from all unrighteousness. Thank you Lord, for allowing me to rededicate my life back to you. In Jesus Name. Amen!

Love Nots

Love Nots

Love Nots

Love Nots

Love Nots

Contact the Author
Ramona Lyons
authorramonalyons@gmail.com
www.ramonalyons.net

Contact the Publisher
KSPublishing LLC.
www.kingdom-scribes.com
Now Accepting Manuscripts

CPSIA information can be obtained
at www.ICGtesting.com
Printed in the USA
JSHW051634220421
13796JS00005B/211